Everyone who likes good food appreciates the essential flavouring qualities of herbs and spices. There can be few people as expert in this subject as Rosemary and John Hemphill, who cultivated and marketed herbs and spices at Somerset Cottage outside Sydney for thirty-five years.

Rosemary Hemphill's Spice Collection is a completely revised and metricated edition of her *Spice and Savour.* All the recipes call for a sweet-smelling spice, in most cases in combination with a fragrant herb or seed, and there is also much fascinating information about the history and uses of these delightful plants and their products.

There are recipes here for all tastes, plain and exotic: good, nourishing, easy dishes for cold nights — Welsh Stew, for instance, or Spinach Soup, Lamb Haricot and Savory Stuffed Leg of Lamb — and dishes that taste as refreshing and delectable as their names. Who could resist Rose Creams, for instance, or Mango Mousse, Chicken Mimosa or Aromatic Sweet Potatoes?

With its great variety of recipes, its many ideas and suggestions and, not least, its charming illustrations by Karen Ball, *Rosemary Hemphill's Spice Collection* will be a source of inspiration and delight in any kitchen.

A companion volume, *Rosemary Hemphill's Herb Collection,* is also available.

Also by Rosemary Hemphill
Fragrance and Flavour
Herbs for all Seasons
Cooking with Herbs and Spices
Rosemary Hemphill's Herb Collection

ANGUS & ROBERTSON PUBLISHERS

Unit 4, Eden Park, 31 Waterloo Road,
North Ryde, NSW, Australia 2113;
94 Newton Road, Auckland 1,
New Zealand; and
16 Golden Square, London W1R 4BN,
United Kingdom

First published in Australia
by Angus & Robertson Publishers in 1964
First published in the United Kingdom
by Angus & Robertson (UK) in 1964
Reprinted 1967, 1971, 1979, 1982, 1984
This revised edition 1989

Copyright © Rosemary Hemphill 1964, 1989

National Library of Australia
Cataloguing-in-publication data.

Hemphill, Rosemary, 1922– .
  Rosemary Hemphill's spice collection

  Includes index.
  ISBN 0 207 16144 5.

  1. Cookery (Herbs). 2. Herbs. 3. Spices. I. Title.
  II. Title: Spice collection. III. Title: Spice and savour:
  cooking with dried herbs and aromatic seeds.
641.6'57

Typeset in 11pt Garamond 3 by Best-set Typesetter Ltd
Printed in Hong Kong

ROSEMARY HEMPHILL'S

SPICE
COLLECTION

ANGUS
& ROBERTSON
PUBLISHERS

for my mother
Doris Goldie

Grateful thanks are expressed to the following people who helped me in one way or another while I was writing this book: Mr and Mrs J. S. Sareen, of the Ministry of External Affairs, New Delhi, for valuable advice on the Indian curry, and for their demonstration of the use of pure silver on the Indian pudding Kheer; Mr and Mrs L. M. Chabot, of the Java Restaurant, Dural, for their helpful discussion about Indonesian curries; Mr Douglas Lamb, of the Douglas Lamb Cellars, Sydney, for his useful comments on the most suitable wines to serve with certain food; my mother, for her generous contributions to my herb library, literature which has been invaluable in research for this book; and Karen Ball, for her imaginative and perceptive illustrations.

Contents

This metric conversion table is included for the convenience of our readers. The equivalents in it are not exact—500 g is slightly more than 1 lb, for example. But this does not matter so long as you follow *either* the metric weights and measures or the imperial in one recipe. Never use a mixture of the two, as the recipe proportions will then be slightly altered. *Note*: A dessertspoon is equivalent to 2 metric teaspoons.

Weights

Ounces/Pounds	Grams
1 ounce	30 g
4 ounces (¼ lb)	125 g
8 ounces (½ lb)	250 g
12 ounces (¾ lb)	375 g
16 ounces (1 lb)	500 g
24 ounces (1½ lb)	750 g
32 ounces (2 lb)	1000 g

Measures

Pints	Millilitres
¼ pint	150 ml
½ pint	300 ml
¾ pint	450 ml
1 pint	600 ml

Temperatures

Fahrenheit (°F)	Celsius (°C)
250	120
300	150
350	175
400	200
425	220
475	245

·SPICE & SAVOUR·

Some herbs, when dried, are known as spices, but these are simply the dried leaves of culinary plants. True spices are aromatic products from various parts of plants usually indigenous to hot countries, where their flavour is at its best. The part required is collected and dried; it may be the buds, bark, berries, fruit, roots, or—as with saffron—the flower stigmas. Nowadays aromatic culinary seeds are generally grouped with spices under that name, and are gathered when ripe from the spent flower-heads of plants.

When dried herbs are used, a much smaller quantity is needed for flavouring than when using herbs picked straight from the garden, for the flavour is more highly concentrated in the dried product. If fresh herbs are called for in a recipe and you do not have them, a fairly general rule to follow is to use one-third of the amount of dried herbs. Usually herbs and spices are meant to complement and bring out the flavour of the dish in which they are being used, not to dominate it, although there are occasions when a greater quantity is called for. I remember eating a friend's delicious apple pie— an old family recipe—with a wonderful pastry dusky with allspice and cinnamon. A tablespoon of allspice and a dessertspoon of cinnamon* are sifted with two cups of self-raising flour and a pinch of salt, then stirred with a packed cup of brown sugar, the whole rubbed together with 125 grams (four ounces) of butter and moistened with one well-beaten egg. (I was told to use a little milk if the mixture was not moist enough.) The pastry should be rolled out thinly, divided into two pieces for lining a greased dish and for covering the sugared, lemon-flavoured apples.

Besides their value as flavouring in food, herbs have, of course, tradition-ally been used in the preparation of medicines. A long time ago man had an affinity with the plant world and a sure, instinctive understanding of it. As Mrs Leyel says in *The Truth About Herbs*, Hipprocrates, the "Father of

* *Level measurements should be used in the recipes in this book unless otherwise stated.*

Medicine", was learned in the preparation of herbs, and of a list left by him of four hundred simples (herbs used medicinally, and medicines made from them), half that number are still in general use today. As well as balm, basil, fennel, and thyme, Hippocrates' list included less familiar, sinister-sounding herbs like hemlock, henbane, and mandragora or mandrake, which had the reputation of shrieking when pulled from the ground.

So, whether we grow herbs, eat them, or take them as medicine, they carry us, if we stop to think about them, far back into history. They have been highly important in trade, and wars have been fought over them. In the Middle Ages they were regarded as necessities, not luxuries, for they helped in the preservation of food, as well as being wanted for medicine. They were difficult to obtain, and had to be brought from the Far East first by sea, then by caravan across the desert to be shipped to the great trading ports of Genoa and Venice; then pack animals carried the precious cargo to waiting merchants in northern Europe who distributed it. Holland, Spain, France, and Portugal have all struggled at various times to control the spice trade.

When we think of herb gardens established in Europe we may call to mind a rich stew, aromatic with thyme and bay leaves, simmering on the stove in a country kitchen agleam with rows of pots and pans, with geraniums blooming on the window-sill, and a glimpse of a well-stocked herb garden through the shining panes; or, farther back into time, we see a fleeting picture of the garden of some medieval monastery, with its orderly rows of plants cloistered by high walls from the outside world. Beyond that again, herbs and spices take us to hot blue Arabian skies; to hundred-gated Thebes humming with life and trade on the banks of the Nile; to the ancient palace of Knossos on Crete, with its murals of saffron-gatherers; and to the Queen of Sheba herself, visiting King Solomon at Jerusalm: ". . . with a very great company, and camels that bear spices, and gold in abundance, and precious stones."

But while we all enjoy the special magic surrounding the legends of herbs and spices, they are valued above all for their practical uses. These have been affirmed in the writings of many civilizations: Egyptian hieroglyphics, the Old Testament, early Greek and Roman documents, Saxon and medieval manuscripts, and the great English herbals of William Turner, John Gerard, and John Parkinson. When reading any history of herbs and spices one is struck by the common sense with which they have been used. Aniseed, for instance, has digestive qualities, and so we read of the Romans finishing their sumptuous feasts with anise cakes. Dill seed has the same attribute, and is often included in old recipes for cooking cabbage to make this vegetable more digestible. And this combination of romance and practicality continues to the present day. Many national or regional dishes rely on a particular herb or spice for their special character: paprika is the spice which imparts to Hungarian goulash its distinctive flavour and colour; chili powder gives Chile con Carne its fire; Spaghetti Bolognese is not complete without oregano; while saffron in Bouillabaisse is traditional.

In the following pages, the plants producing spices, aromatic seeds, and dried herb leaves are given first their common name, then their particular botanical name, and lastly the botanical name of their family group. It is interesting to know that some herbs differing widely in appearance and flavour belong to the same family. For instance, mint, thyme, basil, and rosemary are all members of the large family Labiatae, recognized by their square stems and two-lipped flowers. And tarragon, one of the most popular culinary herbs, belongs to a family (Compositae) which numbers among its members such plants as chrysanthemums, lettuce, the common daisy, and asters: these plants have composite flower-heads made up of tightly clustered florets, hence the botanical name given to the family.

For easy classification and to show their natural grouping, dried herbs, spices, and aromatic seeds popular in cooking are grouped on p. 6:

Herbs

Basil	Mint	Sage
Bay Leaves	Oregano	Savory
Chervil	Parsley	Tarragon
Marjoram	Rosemary	Thyme

Spices

Allspice	Curry Powder	Black Pepper
Cayenne	Ginger	White Pepper
Chili Powder	Mace	Saffron
Cinnamon	Nutmeg	Turmeric
Cloves	Paprika	

Aromatic · Seeds

Aniseed	Cumin Seed	Poppy Seed
Caraway Seed	Dill Seed	Sesame Seed
Cardamom Seed	Fennel Seed	Vanilla Bean
Celery Seed	Juniper Berries	
Coriander Seed	Mustard Seed	

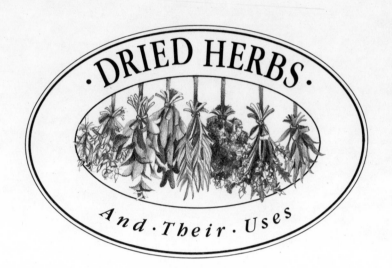

·DRIED HERBS·

And·Their·Uses

Basil

(Ocimum basilicum) Labiatae

A frost-tender annual plant with a delicate, spicy flavour, basil originally came from India, where as *tulasi* it was used in many religious and superstitious rites. Other countries adopted it centuries ago, and it figures prominently in Greek, Italian, and French cooking. There are over forty types of basil, each differing from the others in some way—in the height reached by the plant or perhaps in the size or shape, sometimes even the colour, of the leaves. Three of the better-known kinds are bush basil whose small leaves are hardly bigger than marjoram leaves, sweet basil with much larger leaves, and purple basil with wine-dark foliage which is very decorative but has an inferior aroma and flavour. Because of the size of its leaves and rich perfume, sweet basil is the most popular one for drying.

Basil combines particularly well with tomatoes served in any form, and is also excellent in pasta and rice dishes; with liver, kidneys, and fish; in fricasseed chicken or rabbit, and with eggplant.

Dolmas

An unusual way of serving liver with a green vegetable, both aromatically spiced with basil, is shown in this recipe for stuffed leaves of cabbage, spinach, or, if you have a grape vine, vine leaves.

Cabbage or spinch	1 onion, chopped
500 g (1 lb) lamb's fry	1 cup cooked rice
60 g (2 oz) butter or	2 teaspoons basil
margarine	Several rashers of lean bacon
2 cloves of garlic, finely chopped	2 tablespoons red or white
1 red or green capsicum,	wine, stock, or water
chopped	Salt and pepper

Allow 3 or 4 cabbage, spinach, or vine leaves for each person. Wash the leaves selected for stuffing, cut out any hard stalk, blanch in boiling water for a few minutes, and drain. Soak the lamb's fry in salted water, remove the skin, and chop the meat into small pieces. Melt the butter in a saucepan then soften the onion, garlic, and capsicum in it. Add the meat and allow it to cook gently, turning frequently. Stir in the rice and basil and season with salt and pepper.

Spread out the blanched leaves, put mounds of meat and rice mixture on each one, and roll up into parcels. Place in layers in a casserole with pieces of bacon between the layers and on top. Pour in the liquid and put the casserole lid on. Bake in a slow even (120°C or 250°F) for 1½ to 2 hours. If during the cooking it becomes a little dry, add more liquid.

Basil · and · Tomato · Aspic

A smooth-textured and delicately flavoured aspic. Prepare it a day or so beforehand and keep it chilled in the refrigerator, unmoulding just before serving. Accompany with thin slices of ham, a tossed green salad, and hot rolls.

1200 ml (2 pints) tomato juice	1 dessertspoon basil
1 cup mayonnaise	2 tablespoons lemon juice
3 envelopes, or 3 rounded	1 cup diced celery
dessertspoons, gelatine	1 green capsicum, chopped
½ cup chopped shallots	1 small jar stuffed olives,
3 tablespoons raw or brown	sliced
sugar	Salt and pepper

Soften the gelatine in 1½ cups of the tomato juice. Put the remainder of the juice into a saucepan with the shallots, basil, sugar, and lemon juice. Season with salt and pepper. Bring to the boil, and simmer for a few minutes. Remove from the stove and stir in the dissolved gelatine, then the mayonnaise, celery, capsicum, and olives. Put in a cool place, and when beginning to set pour into a rinsed-out mould. Chill in the refrigerator. Serves 8.

Fish · Roe · Entrée

500 g (½ lb) soft roes   Breadcrumbs
Plain flour   Butter
2 teaspoons basil   Salt and pepper
150 ml (¼ pint) cream

Roll the roes in seasoned plain flour and lay them in a buttered ovenproof dish. Sprinkle with the basil, add the cream, top with breadcrumbs, and dot with butter. Bake in a moderate oven (175°C or 350°F) for 10 to 15 minutes. Serve hot.

Bay

(Laurus nobilis) Lauraceae

The bay or laurel tree, whose leaves were once made into wreaths to crown the heroes of ancient Greece and Rome, is native to Mediterranean areas. It is grown in countries all over the world, for it is decorative, and a pleasing aromatic scent is imparted to food by the dark green leaves. An oil used in herbal medicine is extracted from the leaves and berries.

Although a bay tree will grow to grand proportions, it may be cut back periodically without any adverse effect. It makes an attractive standard tree when encouraged to grow on one central stem by snipping off any laterals or suckers, with the top rounded into a large glossy green ball; the formal shape of the leaves gives bay trees cultivated in this way an extremely elegant appearance. They are sometimes seen growing in tubs at the entrance doors of restaurants and hotels, and in the miniature gardens of penthouses.

Bay leaves may be used straight from the tree, or dried; when freshly dried they retain their flavour particularly well. A bay leaf or two is included in countless recipes: a leaf is part of a *bouquet garni*, the other herbs usually being a spray each of thyme, marjoram, and parsley. Bay leaves are included in soups, stews, and casseroles, in the making of stock, when cooking corned beef, salted mutton, pickled pork, tongue, poultry, and fish. A bay leaf was often used by our grandmothers to flavour milk puddings.

Welsh · Stew

My mother's recipe for Welsh stew, given to her by her mother, is succulent with meat and gravy, and fragrant with thyme and bay leaves. The stock may be made with beef cubes.

Cut 1 kg (2 lb) beef into neat pieces and put in a casserole with 900 ml (1½ pints) stock. Bring to the boil, then simmer for ¾ hour. Add the white part of a bunch of leeks, well washed and cut up, a turnip cut into dice, 2 bay leaves, a spray of thyme, season with salt and pepper, and add a lump of sugar. Let all stew gently for about 1 hour. Serve in the casserole.

Fish · Special

Another excellent dish from my mother's recipe book.

Roll fillets of fish prettily and place them in a buttered fire-proof dish with one or two bay leaves. Over the fillets pour a glass of white wine and then sprinkle them with a layer of chopped chives or shallots. Add a few more pieces of butter and cook in a closed dish long and slowly. If allowed to get cold, the fish will be surrounded by a rich jelly.

Rice · and · Treacle · Pudding

Here is a plain but nourishing milk pudding from the family recipe book. It is popular with children.

In an ovenproof dish blend together 2 scant tablespoons rice and 1 tablespoon golden syrup. Gradually incorporate 600 ml (1 pint) milk. Dot with butter, and lay a bay leaf on top. Bake in a slow oven (135°C or 275°F) for about 1½ hours. May be eaten hot or cold, with cream.

Chervil

(Anthriscus cerefolium) Umbelliferae

Chervil is native to eastern Europe, self-sowing easily in cool climates. Usually treated as an annual, like parsley which it closely resembles, it is sometimes described as a biennial; the leaves, however, are fern-like and finely cut, and the flavour is entirely different, being delicately scented with aniseed. When dried it holds its aroma and green colour well. Even if chervil were grown, or kept in its dried state, only for adding to creamed potato or scrambled egg, it would be worthwhile. However, the uses of this herb are manifold, and it makes an attractive addition to many kinds of food. It may be sprinkled on soups, salads, cooked vegetables, sauces, and savoury soufflés, and on fish, poultry, and game dishes.

Spinach · Soup

1200 ml (2 pints) beef stock	One or more 4-minute eggs for
600 ml (1 pint) cooked	each person
spinach, sieved or put	A little cream
through a blender	Chervil
	Salt and pepper

Put the pureed spinach into a saucepan with the beef stock. Heat, adding salt and pepper to taste. Have ready the eggs which have been boiled and shelled. Serve the hot soup in individual bowls with a whole egg, a dessertspoon of cream, and a generous sprinking of chervil.

Seafood · Salad

3 cups fish, cooked and flaked	1 cucumber, peeled and diced
1 cup shelled prawns	1/2 cup mayonnaise
1 bottle oysters, drained	1 tablespoon lemon juice
1 dessertspoon chopped chives	1 tablespoon thick cream
(or 2 dessertspoons chopped	Chervil
shallots)	Salt and pepper
2 tomatoes, peeled and diced	

Toss all ingredients together (except the chervil) and chill in the refrigerator. Serve in a bowl lined with crisp lettuce leaves, strewing the top until green with the chervil.

Iced · Avocado · and · Chervil

This makes a refreshing accompaniment to a main dish. Slice 2 peeled and stoned avocados lengthwise into slender pieces. Marinate in lemon juice seasoned with salt and freshly ground pepper. To serve, sprinkle with plenty of chervil and arrange on a bed of cracked ice.

Marjoram

(Origanum majorana) Labiatae

This is a perennial plant, native to southern Europe but introduced long ago to other parts of the world. There are many different kinds, the best known being the ancient pot marjoram, wild marjoram, "Dittany of Crete", and knotted marjoram. They are all steeped in legend: one belief was that marjoram brought peace and happiness.

Except for wild marjoram, which is better known as oregano, knotted or sweet marjoram is the kind used most widely today for culinary purposes. (Oregano, a valuable cooking herb, is dealt with separately in another chapter.) The tight appearance of the milk-white flower-heads and buds gives knotted marjoram its popular name; although a perennial it is usually treated as an annual in extremely cold climates. The delicately scented, soft, greyish leaves have long found favour with cooks, and the sweet aroma of this herb was also valued for strewing on floors and for putting in pot-pourri and

sweet-bags. Marjoram is blended with thyme, sage, parsley, and other seasoning herbs to make a delicious mixture for stuffings and for flavouring savoury dishes, but it is sometimes used singly, for its delicate aroma is more acceptable to some people than the strongly perfumed blended herbs. It is used to flavour cream sauces for fish, with shellfish, and in vegetable cookery. It also imparts a subtle flavour to rabbit.

Summer · Vegetable · Tart

Marjoram is used in a lightly scented seasoning for this tart, which may be eaten at luncheon or supper or taken on a picnic.

Rich short-crust pastry

Sift 1½ cups self-raising flour and a pinch of salt into a bowl, rub in 125 g (¼ lb) butter until the mixture is crumbly, add ¼ cup very cold water and a squeeze of lemon juice, and mix to a dry dough.

Filling

1 cup cooked peas, 2 cooked carrots finely sliced, 1 cup cooked potatoes finely sliced, 2 tablespoons chopped shallots, 3 eggs, ½ cup cream, 2 teaspoons marjoram, some salt and pepper.

Roll the pastry out thinly and line a buttered 20 cm (8 inch) shallow pie-dish with it. Prick the pastry all over, and fill with the vegetables, arranging them attractively. Mix the eggs, cream, and marjoram together, seasoning with salt and pepper, and pour carefully over the vegetables. Bake in a moderate oven (190°C or 375°F) until set—about 30 minutes. Serve the tart warm or cold, decorated with a few fresh marjoram leaves.

Oysters · Bercy

3 doz. oysters, drained
2 heaped tablespoons finely
  chopped shallots
60 g (2 oz) butter
1 cup white wine
1 dessertspoon lemon juice

2 teaspoons marjoram
1 scant tablespoon plain flour
1 cup thin cream
Salt and pepper
Ground nutmeg

Soften the shallots in butter without browning. Add the wine, lemon juice, and marjoram, season with salt and pepper, and simmer over low heat until reduced a little. Mix the flour and cream together, add to the sauce and stir until thickened. Remove from heat, stir the oysters into the sauce, and spoon into ramekins or scallop shells. Sprinkle lightly with nutmeg, put into the oven, and heat through for 5 to 8 minutes. Serve hot with small squares of brown bread-and-butter.

Whitebait, scallops, or sliced fish fillets may be used in place of oysters. Sauce Bercy may also be served over asparagus, sliced avocado pear, sautéed mushrooms or with delicately textured grilled meat.

Veal · in · Apple · Juice

750 g (1½ lb) veal steak
2¼ cups apple juice
2 tablespoons plain flour
2 teaspoons marjoram
2 teaspoons mustard seed

1 crumbled bay leaf
1 onion, finely chopped
1 clove of garlic, finely chopped
A few peppercorns
Salt

Cut the veal into strips, roll them in flour and place them in an ovenproof dish. Sprinkle with half each of the marjoram, mustard seed, crumbled bay leaf, onion, garlic, and peppercorns, with a little salt. Repeat, then pour the apple juice over. Cover, and bake in a moderate oven (175°C or 350°F) for 1 to 1½ hours.

Mint

(Mentha spicata) Labiatae

Mint has been grown and cultivated for many centuries, and is one of the plants mentioned in the Bible. The kinds now in existence make a very long list, and their leaves are of many aromas and shapes. A few interesting mints with definite flavours of their own, all suitably named, are eau-de-Cologne mint, applemint, peppermint, and spearmint. The hardiest and most useful mint for drying is the vigorous curly-leaved spearmint.

It has been found that leaves from a mint plant grown in the sun have a better flavour than those from a more lush-looking plant grown in the shade; but when cultivated in full sunlight, mint must be watered more frequently. It is well worth the small amount of extra work.

Mint may be dried on racks or in bunches hung in an airy place. The leaves should then be stripped from the stems and rubbed through a fine sieve. After having been treated in this way, 3 kg (7 lb) of fresh mint is reduced to about 500 g (1 lb). The flavour is much stronger than that of fresh mint, of course, and only a small amount should be used at a time.

Mint has many qualities, one of which is that it helps the digestion: peppermint tea is particularly good for this purpose, and it gives one a sense of relaxation and well-being at the same time. Mint has the reputation of repelling fleas, and it was used as a strewing herb in the Middle Ages. This herb with the warm, vital scent is used in numerous favourite recipes: in iced tea and fruit salads; with peas and new potatoes; as mint julep, mint jelly, and mint sauce—to mention just a few.

Mint sauce for roast lamb is made in less than a minute by putting a dessertspoon of dried mint into a small jug with sugar, vinegar, and hot water.

A teaspoon or two of dried mint may be sprinkled on tomatoes just before they are grilled, fried, or baked.

Shake a little dried or chopped fresh mint into scrambled egg, mashed potato, or buttered vegetables before serving.

Mint is supposed to prevent milk from curdling. Eleanour Sinclair Rohde, in *A Garden of Herbs*, quotes this old recipe from *The Good Housewife's Handmaid*, 1588: "Mintes put into milk, it neyther suffereth the same to curde, nor to become thick, insomuch that layed in curded milke, this would bring the same thinne againe."

French-Style · Peas

Shell 750 g (1½ lb) fresh young peas, or use a packet (250 g to 375 g) of good-quality frozen peas. Wash the heart of a lettuce and arrange it in a saucepan, add the peas, 1 dessertspoon chopped spring onions, 2 teaspoons dried mint, a pinch each of salt and sugar, and a few pieces of butter. Put the lid on the saucepan and place over a low heat. Shake the pan frequently at first; after a few minutes you will see that the peas are cooking in the moisture from the lettuce and the melted butter. Five to seven minutes is usually sufficient cooking time. Serve the peas and spring onions with the cooked lettuce, which is delicate and delicious.

Mint · and · Marshmallow Custard

This simple milk pudding may be eaten either hot or cold. The marshmallows become caramelized, and the mint counteracts any tendency to over-sweetness.

With a fork beat together in an ovenproof dish 3 eggs and 1 tablespoon sugar. Gradually mix in 600 ml (1 pint) milk. Dust with 2 teaspoons dried mint and float about 24 marshmallows on top. Stand the dish in a shallow container of hot water, and place in a moderate oven (175°C or 350°F) to bake until set.

Mint · and · Cheese · Dressing

To make this delicious dressing for baked potatoes, take 2 teaspoons dried mint and 1 packet of cream cheese, and pound a small clove of garlic. Mix thoroughly. Wash and dry some potatoes, rub them well with vegetable oil, and bake in a hot oven (200°C or 400°F) for 1 hour. Remove the potatoes from the oven, slit the tops with a knife and squeeze their sides slightly. Spoon the cheese dressing over them and serve hot.

Oregano

(*Origanum vulgare*) *Labiatae*

Oregano is native of the Mediterranean and is the most pungently hot of all the popular culinary herbs. It is one of the marjorams, but has more vigour in its growing habit, flavour, and smell than the others of this family. The name *Origanum* comes from Greek words meaning "joy of the mountains", which is very suitable because it grows in such a lively way, the bees clustering round the small white flowers when they appear, and the leaves seeming to absorb every ray of sunshine and clean, fresh air. Oregano is one of the most widely known herbs and is an ingredient of many classic national dishes. It is always included in Italian spaghetti dishes and in pizzas, in Chile con Carne from Mexico, and in numerous Spanish sauces (often under the name of wild marjoram). It is also used in guacamole, in tomato cookery, with mushroom dishes, with meat (especially veal and beef), and in a cream sauce to be poured over boiled white onions.

Spaghetti · Bolognese

This method of serving Spaghetti Bolognese is rather different, and very tasty.

500 g (1 lb) minced steak	1 cup stock (may be made with
60 g (2 oz) butter	a beef cube)
1 clove of garlic, finely chopped	Salt and pepper
1 onion, peeled and chopped	2 teaspoons oregano
300 ml (½ pint) tomato puree	250g (½ lb) spaghetti
or 500 g (1 lb) fresh, peeled	
tomatoes	

Garnish

1 tomato, sliced	2 rashers rindless bacon
1 capsicum, sliced	2 teaspoons dried parsley
1 cup finely grated cheese	

Heat the shortening in a heavy saucepan, and fry the meat, garlic, and onion until brown. Add the tomato puree or the fresh tomatoes, and the stock, salt, pepper, and oregano. Cover, and simmer gently for 30 minutes.

In the meantime cook the spaghetti in plenty of boiling, salted water until it is soft (about 20 minutes), moving it occasionally with a fork so that the strands do not stick. Place it in a colander to drain, then pour hot water through it.

Take a greased casserole dish, put a layer of meat and sauce in the bottom, then half the spaghetti, another layer of meat and sauce, and finish with the rest of the spaghetti. To garnish, place the sliced tomato and capsicum over the top, sprinkle with the cheese, then the bacon (which has been cut into several pieces, each piece rolled up neatly and secured with a toothpick). Bake in a moderate oven (175°C or 350°F) until the cheese and bacon are cooked. Sprinkle the parsley over the top and bring the dish to the table.

Olives · Oregano

When black or green olives are steeped in a marinade of oil, herbs, and spices they acquire an added flavour and a mellow smoothness. Drain the olives for a short time before using them.

Prick 500 g (1 lb) olives with a silver fork and put them in a screw-top jar, add 1 cup vegetable oil, ½ teaspoon thyme, 1 teaspoon crushed peppercorns, and 2 teaspoons oregano. Top up with oil if necessary, cover, shake well and put into the refrigerator. Leave for at least 2 days, and use as required. Spear on wooden picks, or stone the olives and serve on vine leaves for lunch with black bread, two or three cheeses, and a light red wine. Especially delicious if eaten out of doors in the sunshine.

Quiche · Lorraine

Line a buttered pie-dish with short-crust pastry (page 16). Prick all over. Remove the rind from 250 g (½ lb) bacon, cut into squares, and fry or grill until crisp. Place 3 or 4 whole thin slices of Cheddar cheese (obtainable in packets containing about 8 slices) on the pastry, then half the bacon and 1 teaspoon oregano. Repeat once more. Make a rich custard with 300 ml (½ pint) cream and 2 eggs, season with salt and pepper, and pour it over the cheese. Bake in a moderate oven (190°C or 375°F) for 30 minutes or until cooked. When cool, strew the top with stoned black olives.

Parsley

(*Petroselinum crispum*) *Umbelliferae*

Parsley has been known all over the world for so many centuries that its origins are obscure, but it is thought to have first come from Sardinia. There are several kinds, among them curled parsley, plain-leaved, fern-leaved, and turnip-rooted parsley. "Italian" parsley has plain leaves and a parsnip-like root which is useful for flavouring soups and stews; the seed germinates very easily—in fact under most conditions the plant self-sows each year.

There have been more legends and superstitions about parsley than about any other herb, and many have come down to the present day. One belief is that if the seeds are sown on Good Friday they will bring happiness and good fortune.

It has been known since early times that this herb possesses healthful properties. In *The Truth About Herbs* Mrs C. F. Leyel writes: "Parsley juice is rich in vitamin C and carotene and in most of the valuable organic salts. It is a useful general tonic, and acts specifically as a tonic for the kidneys."

Parsley is used for garnishing all kinds of food. Fried in butter, sprigs of parsley are a classic accompaniment to fish. It is added chopped to white sauce, mashed potato, scrambled egg, and countless other dishes.

When people are unable to grow parsley because of climatic conditions or lack of garden space, it is sadly missed, but dried parsley is an excellent substitute. If it is dried quickly and carefully its colour and flavour in the food are indistinguishable from that of fresh parsley. So when your parsley grows in abundance, dry some of it—it will come in useful when this flavouring is wanted in a hurry, or when the garden yield is small. To dry it, spread sprigs on racks, or hang them in bunches in a warm, airy room. Parsley may also be dried quickly in a warm (*not* hot) oven. When crisp, rub through a sieve and seal in airtight containers. Use it for sprinkling on top of soups, for putting in mashed potato, all eggs dishes, and in dumplings for a casserole or stew. Use it in sauces, mayonnaise and for parsley butter. Dip the tops of lemon wedges in dried parsley for an appetising garnish.

Noodles · and · Mushrooms

500 g (1 lb) noodles, any shape	500 g (1 lb) mushrooms, peeled and sliced
1/2 teacup oil	250 g (1/2 lb) bacon, grilled or fried, and cut into pieces
2 tomatoes, peeled and chopped	
3 cloves of garlic, finely cut up	1 dessertspoon dried parsley
2 tablespoons chopped capsicum	Salt and pepper
1 onion, chopped	Grated Parmesan cheese

Heat the oil in a heavy saucepan and add the tomato, onion, garlic, capsicum, and mushrooms. Cook gently for 10 to 15 minutes, then add the bacon and parsley, with salt and pepper to taste. While preparing the mushroom mixture, have the noodles cooking in a quantity of boiling salted water, stirring them occasionally to prevent sticking. When soft, drain them well. Put into a warmed dish, cover with the hot mushroom mixture, and sprinkle generously with grated Parmesan cheese.

Parsley · Butter

For grills, fish, and baked-jacket potatoes. Other herb butters may be made the same.

Soften 125 g (¼ lb) butter with a fork and work into it a few drops of lemon juice and 2 teaspoons dried parsley. Spread on a saucer and place in the refrigerator to harden. Cut into cubes and put them on a dish to be handed round at the table, or place cubes on the food just before serving it.

Lamb · Haricot

Have a leg of lamb cut right through into circles by the butcher. The meat is trimmed of fat and put into a large casserole with chopped onions, garlic, and tomatoes, a seasoning of salt, a few peppercorns, and a little stock. Bake with the lid on in a slow oven (120° to 150°C or 250° to 300°F) for 3 hours. Twenty minutes before serving, add 2 cups of cooked haricot beans. Finally, strew dried parsley liberally over it.

Rosemary

(Rosmarinus officinalis) Labiatae

This Mediterranean evergreen herb has mist-blue flowers that are loved by the bees. Rosemary was highly esteemed by the ancient Greeks and Romans, who introduced it to other countries. It was known to the Saxons and is referred to in one of the earliest herbals, the Saxon "Leech Book of Bald". It achieved great popularity in Tudor England for culinary, medicinal, and decorative reasons, and in those days was used for topiary work and was espaliered against walls. Shakespeare, Spenser, and many other poets have written about it. The wood of rosemary was used to make lutes and carpenter's rules.

There are several types: a rare gilded-leaved plant; a double-flowering kind; another with white flowers; one with broad leaves; a rosemary with horizontal branches which is valuable for rockery work; and the well-known bushy, upright rosemary which is the type most frequently used for

seasoning. With the attractive symmetry of its narrow leaves and its rather stiff growing habit, this type makes a decorative hedge of medium height.

There is a great deal of herb lore surrounding rosemary: the French believed that the flowers rekindled lost energy, and they sometimes burnt branches of the bush for incense. It was also supposed to ward off black magic; it figured prominently on happy occasions such as weddings and banquets; and sprigs of rosemary to this day symbolize remembrance and friendship.

The bracing and tonic effect of the leaves has always been valued. In *A Garden of Herbs* Eleanour Sinclair Rohde quotes from an old herbal: "Also if thou be feeble boyle the leaves in cleane water and washe thyself and thou shalt wax shiny." Among its many other virtues, rosemary stimulates the scalp and helps to relieve nervous headaches.

The name rosemary means "dew of the sea", and although the plant is hardy and will grow practically anywhere—except through the severest winters, when it should be brought indoors—it flourishes best and has more flavour when grown near the sea.

When dried, the leaves become crisp and brittle, and are easily crumbled or chopped. The pungent scent of rosemary enhances certain food, particularly lamb, veal, pork and beef. When added to a scone mixture it gives the scones a delicious flavour; it may often be used instead of thyme, and is excellent in pea soup, minestrone, spinach soup, and in casseroles and stews, or added to the water for boiling pickled pork.

Buttered · Cabbage · Spines and · Rosemary

A new and delicious vegetable was introduced to us by my aunt and uncle when they were on a visit from England: in fact, two vegetables are made from one. The pale-green "spines" are cut from the leaves of a cabbage with a pair of sharp kitchen scissors, giving a mound of crisp stalks and another of soft leaves with no stalks. Wrap these leaves in foil and put in the refrigerator for another occasion (when they may be shredded finely and steamed for a few minutes with a knob of butter). Put the cabbage spines or stalks into a saucepan with water and a little salt, bring to the boil, and simmer until they are tender (this may take from 20 to 30 minutes). Drain the stalks and pour over them a mixture of melted butter and 2 teaspoons of finely chopped or crumbled rosemary.

Beef · and · Tomatoes

In this hearty dish from the Mediterranean, the juices from the meat and vegetables mingle with the herbs and wine to form a savoury and aromatic sauce.

750 g (1½ lb) shin of beef, roughly cut up
3 rashers of bacon, cut in squares
1 glass white or red wine
4 tomatoes, peeled
2 cloves of garlic, sliced
2 onions, peeled and sliced
1 dessertspoon chopped rosemary
1 bay leaf
10 juniper berries, crushed
Salt and pepper

Put the meat into a casserole and cover it with the squares of bacon, then add the remaining ingredients. Bake with the lid on in a slow oven (120° to 150°C or 250° to 300°F) for 3 to 4 hours.

Rosemary · Scones

I have often served these scones to people who are interested in the unique flavour that herbs give to everyday food. As there could be nothing more everyday than scones, and as the recipe has been so popular, here it is.

2 cups self-raising flour
A pinch each of salt and sugar
1 tablespoon butter

1 tablespoon finely chopped
rosemary
¾ cup milk

Sift the flour with salt and sugar, rub in the butter, add the rosemary, then the milk. Mix to a soft dough, roll lightly, and cut into squares. Place the squares close together on a greased and floured baking sheet, and bake in a hot oven (220°C or 425°F) for about 15 minutes.

Dried rosemary may be moistened first before chopping it; or crumble it between the fingers.

Sage

(Salvia officinalis) Labiatae

Aromatic sage is a perennial plant native to Mediterranean countries, the Romans having brought it to the lands they conquered. Several kinds are known today, each differing in the colour, flavour, and shape of the leaves. There is a sage with purple-tinged leaves, a pineapple-flavoured sage, a white-flowering and a pink-flowering sage. As the purple-flowering grey-leaved sage is used most frequently, it is the one described here. Sun-loving, it will thrive for many years in a well-drained, sheltered position, but will wither and die if the soil and situation are not to its liking. The healthiest sage plant I have seen was over five years old; it was over a metre (three feet) high, and was growing in front of a sunny brick wall.

Sage is believed to have properties that are conducive to longevity. The old herbalists had great respect for it, and country folk included it in their daily diet. It is interesting to read old recipes for sage wine, sage tea, sage cream, and éven sage tobacco. This herb was sometimes used as a flavouring in the making of bread, also of cheese: and there is at least one cheese on the market today that is flecked with sage. The traditional Mixed Herbs contain sage as well as thyme and marjoram, and it is an ingredient in the classic stuffing for roast duck known as Sage and Onion Stuffing.

Halved, buttered tomatoes piled with small mounds of scented, dried sage and baked until tender, go well with grilled pork chops and apple sauce.

A sage-cheese spread is simply made by beating 3 teaspoons of dried sage and a few drops of lemon juice into 125 g (4 oz) cream cheese.

Rub a joint of meat with dried sage before roasting it. Try sage as a seasoning for meat rissoles, meat loaf, cheese dishes, eggs and fish.

Isabelle's · Sage and · Cheese · Omelet

1 cup grated Cheddar cheese	1 dessertspoon grated onion
1 cup milk	2 teaspoons chopped sage
2 eggs, separated	Salt and pepper
1 cup soft breadcrumbs	

This is an excellent luncheon or supper dish.

Warm the milk, and add it to the beaten egg yolks and other ingredients (except the egg whites). Add salt and pepper. Allow the mixture to stand for 1 hour. Fold in the whipped egg whites. Bake in a buttered dish in a fairly moderate oven (175°C or 350°F) for 30 minutes.

Sage · Bread

This sage-flavoured bread is well worth the small amount of time and effort spent in preparing it. As it is a particularly quick method, it could become a winter standby to accompany roast meat, casseroles, and thick stews, or for Sunday night supper with bowls of hot soup. It is delicious with Camembert and coffee.

15 g (½ oz) dry yeast
3 tablespoons warm water
500 g (1 lb) plain flour
1 teaspoon salt
2 dessertspoons dried sage
1 teaspoon allspice

1 teaspoon celery seed
1 dessertspoon sugar
1 scant cup warm milk
30 g (1 oz) butter
1 lightly beaten egg

Dissolve the yeast in the warm water. Sift the flour and salt into a bowl, and mix in the sage, allspice, celery seed, and sugar. Form a well in the centre and pour into it the warm (not hot) milk in which the butter has been melted, then the egg and the dissolved yeast. Mix lightly, turn out onto a floured surface, and knead. Put into a greased bowl, cover with a small blanket, and leave in a warm place to rise for 1 hour. Turn out onto a floured surface once more. (In cold weather, first stand the warmed bowl on the table for a few minutes so that there is not too great a drop in temperature for the dough when it is turned out onto the board.) Knead and shape into a cottage loaf or two small loaves, place on a greased baking sheet, and allow to stand for 15 minutes. Bake in a hot oven (220°C or 425°F) for about 30 minutes. If the top is browning too much, cover with a sheet of tinfoil and reduce oven temperature by 30°C (50°F).

Sage · Hair · Tonic

Here is an old "receipt" from *Lotions and Potions,* a collection of their ancestors' recipes compiled by members of the Women's Institute, England.

Take 1 tablespoonful each of tea and of dried sage. Put into a 2 lb (1 kg) jam jar, cover with boiling water, and simmer for 2 hours. Cool and strain. Rub into the scalp four or five times a week. Gradually greyness will disappear, and hair becomes dark brown. Will keep for a week; add 1 tablespoonful of rum, gin, or eau-de-Cologne for longer keeping

Sage · Tea

If you have sage and lemon balm growing, here is a wholesome old beverage quoted in *A Garden of Herbs* by Eleanour Sinclair Rohde from *The New Art of Cookery,* by Richard Briggs (many years Cook at the Globe Tavern, Fleet Street, The White Hart Tavern, Holborn, and at the Temple Coffee House, 1788): "Take a little sage, a little Balm, put it into a pan, slice a Lemon, peel and all, a few knobs of sugar, one glass of white wine; pour on these two or three quarts (3000 ml) of boiling water; cover it, and drink when thirsty. When you think it strong enough of the herbs take them out otherwise it will make it bitter."

To · Whiten · the · Teeth

Rub with sage leaves. This hint also came from *Lotions and Potions*.

Savory

(Satureia montana) Labiatae

Savory is another native plant of the Mediterranean countries, but like numbers of other well-known herbs it is grown and enjoyed in many other parts of the world. The Romans are believed to have introduced it to England, and it was so well liked that it was one of the herbs taken by the early settlers to America.

There are several kinds of savory, the two best known being summer savory, an annual, and winter savory, a perennial. The flavour is essentially

the same in both—peppery and aromatic, with the elusive scent of rosemary and the pungency of sage. The sturdy evergreen bushes of winter savory make an attractive low hedge for a herb garden, and it was put to great use in Tudor days for this purpose and for knot gardens and dwarf shrub mazes. Eleanour Sinclair Rohde says in *Herbs and Herb Gardening*: "Hyll, in his *Proffitable Arte of Gardening* (1568), gives a plan for a dwarf shrub maze 'and it may eyther be set with Isope and Tyme or with winter Savory and Tyme. For these do well endure all the winter through grene'".

Savory retains its flavour well when dried, and is a most useful herb. Traditionally known as "the bean herb", it should accompany all bean dishes, just as mint goes with peas, and basil with tomatoes. Savory with chopped chives and parsley makes an excellent stuffing for duck. It is a pleasant accompaniment for lamb, pork, and veal, and gives a delightfully different flavour to tomato sauce.

Savory · and · Grape · Juice Jelly

A mellow and fragrant jelly to eat with turkey, ham, and other meat dishes, equally delicious on buttered hot rolls and scones. The glowing colour reminds me of how the jelly described by Flora Thompson in *Lark Rise to Candleford* must have looked when ready to eat—jelly that was strained and sweetened and laced with port, sufficient to colour it a deep ruby, and cleared with eggshells, and strained again, then poured into a flannel jellybag and hung from a hook all night to let its contents ooze through, then poured into a mould and allowed yet one more night in which to set.

This recipe is delicious, and it is very easy to make.

1 bottle dark grape juice	*125 g (4 oz) powdered pectin*
2 dessertspoons dried savory	*3 cups sugar*
	Juice of a lemon

Heat the grape juice and savory together, then add the pectin and bring to the boil. Add the sugar and lemon juice and boil for 2 minutes, stirring all the time. Remove from the stove, skim, and seal into small jars immediately.

Savory · Tomato · Sauce

This is an excellent sauce with grills.

Peel and chop 500 g (1 lb) ripe tomatoes and simmer them in a saucepan with 1 finely chopped onion, 2 teaspoons dried savory, and 1 cup water, adding salt and pepper to taste. When cooked, rub through a sieve. Melt 60 g (2 oz) butter, blend in 1 heaped tablespoon plain flour, and gradually add the sauce. Stir until thickened. Bottle.

Savory · Stuffed Leg · of · Lamb

1 small leg of lamb, boned
1 cup soft breadcrumbs
2 teaspoons dried savory
1 dessertspoon chopped white onion
1 clove of garlic, finely chopped
6 juniper berries, crushed
A few pieces of butter
1 cup red or white wine
125 g (¼ lb) butter or margarine, melted
Salt and pepper

Mix together the breadcrumbs, savory, onion, garlic, crushed juniper berries, and the pieces of butter, adding salt and pepper to taste. Stuff the leg, fasten it with skewers, and put it into a baking dish with the wine and the melted butter. Bake in a moderate oven (175° to 190°C or 350° to 375°F) for 1 to 1½ hours, basting frequently. Add a little more wine if necessary. To serve, lift the leg onto a hot dish and pour pan juices over it. Surround with well-drained boiled potatoes coated with butter and chopped parsley.

Tarragon

(Artemisia dracunculus) Compositae

This perennial herb is native to Europe and parts of Asia. There are two accepted culinary types, known as French tarragon and Russian tarragon. While the latter sets seed and is easy to cultivate, it is generally thought that the flavour is not as good as that of French tarragon, which is prized by cooks. The particular aroma of French tarragon suits certain food to perfection; the plant, however, is usually grown only from cuttings or root division, and hardly ever sets seed. Soil and climatic conditions change the taste of the leaves considerably, even when cuttings are taken from a parent plant with an excellent flavour.

Tarragon belongs to the same family as those famous and interesting herbs wormwood, southernwood, cudweed, and mugwort; these are all artemisias, and have long been valued for their medicinal properties. Wormwood is an ingredient in the making of the French liqueur absinthe, and it is also used in certain medicines. Cudweed was called Live-for-ever and Herbe Impious, the reason for the last name being given in Gerard's Herbal (1597): "...those floures which appeare first...are overtopt by other floures, which come on younger branches, and grow higher as children seeking to overgrow or overtop their parents (as many wicked children do), for which cause it hath been called 'Herbe impious'". Mugwort has a fascinating history in early folklore and was regarded as having mystic qualities. Nearly every English cottage garden had a bush of southernwood, also known as Lad's Love or Old Man; its peculiar antiseptic smell repels moths, and it has medicinal virtues as well. Of this unusual and appealing plant Edward Thomas writes in his poem "Old Man":

> Old Man, or Lad's-love—in the name there's nothing
> To one that knows not Lad's-love, or Old Man,
> The hoar-green feathery herb, almost a tree,
> Growing with rosemary and lavender.
> Even to one that knows it well, the names
> Half decorate, half perplex, the thing it is:
> At least, what that is clings not to the names
> In spite of time. And yet I like the names.

Tarragon is the most palatable of the artemisias. It is tartly aromatic, and its uses in the kitchen are many. The leaves when steeped in white vinegar impart a fragrant bouquet. It is usual to add a little chopped tarragon to such sauces as Hollandaise, Béarnaise, and Tartare. Tarragon gives chicken stuffing a delightfully different flavour. It is excellent in fish and shellfish dishes, in veal and rabbit dishes, with chicken livers, and in chicken or fish soups. It may be added to sour cream sauces, mayonnaise, and French dressing. When using the dried herb, chop it finely and begin with 1 teaspoon unless otherwise stated in the recipe: a little more can then be added according to taste.

Hollandaise · Sauce

Hollandaise and Béarnaise sauce are similar in composition. Other well-known sauces, such as Mousseline and Choron, are based on these two, the ingredients that make the variation being added at the end.

There are several methods of making Hollandaise, but I have found the following recipe the most satisfactory. It is important to have all ingredients to hand. If you haven't a double saucepan, a bowl stood in gently boiling water will do instead.

2 egg yolks	*125 g (¼ lb) butter*
1 tablespoon cream	*1 teaspoon chopped tarragon*
1 dessertspoon lemon juice	*Salt and pepper*
1 tablespoon water	

Into a small bowl within easy reach of the stove put the yolks, cream, lemon juice, and water, with salt and pepper to taste. When water is boiling gently in the bottom half of a double saucepan, melt the butter in the top half, then with a wire whisk beat in the contents of the small bowl. Continue beating until the mixture thickens, then remove immediately from the heat, beating a little longer to prevent curdling (if this happens, quickly beat in a few drops of cold water and another egg yolk). Add the tarragon.

Hollandaise sauce should be served lukewarm. It may be poured into the cavity of ripe, stoned avocado pears for an entrée. It is delicious with asparagus, young beans, grilled fish, and other finely textured food.

Chicken · Livers · in · Wine

750 g (1½ lb) chicken livers	*2 teaspoons chopped tarragon*
125 g (¼ lb) butter	*1 tablespoon plain flour*
2 cloves of garlic, finely chopped	*300 ml (½ pint) red or white wine*
1 teaspoon dried marjoram	*Salt and pepper*

Wash the chicken livers, cut in half, and simmer gently in the butter with the garlic until cooked. Add the tarragon, marjoram, and flour, season with salt and pepper, and turn the livers until the flour browns. Gradually add the wine, stirring until the gravy is smooth and thickened. Serve with boiled rice.

Chicken · Mimosa

Steam a chicken until the flesh is tender. Keep the chicken stock for making the sauce. Remove the flesh from the bones while the bird is still hot, and cut into thin slices. Make a stuffing by mixing together 2 cups soft breadcrumbs, 3 teaspoons seasoning herbs, 1 dessertspoon chopped tarragon, 1 dessertspoon chopped shallots, and a little grated lemon rind, adding salt and pepper to taste. Spread this mixture in the bottom of a buttered fireproof dish and lay the chicken slices on it.

Make Sauce Suprême by melting in a saucepan 125 g (¼ lb) butter, blending in ½ cup plain flour, and gradually adding 900 ml (1½ pints) chicken stock. Stir until thickened. Lightly beat together 5 eggs, 150 ml (¼ pint) cream, and a sprinkling of salt and pepper. Pour a little of the thickened chicken liquid from the saucepan onto these eggs, then add this to the contents of the saucepan. Allow to cook for a few minutes (do not boil), stirring all the time. Now pour the sauce over the chicken pieces in the fireproof dish. Bake in a slow oven (150°C or 300°F) for about 45 minutes, or until the sauce has set. Sprinkle the top with the sieved yolks of 2 hard-boiled eggs.

This dish may be made in advance and gently heated through in the oven before being served hot with French-style peas and Saffron Risotto. The fruity flavour of white burgundy is an ideal companion for this rich and savoury dish.

Tarragon · Vinegar

If you have no fresh tarragon growing, steep 1 heaped tablespoon of dried tarragon leaves in 1 pint of white vinegar. Leave for at least 2 weeks before using. The tarragon need not be strained off.

Thyme

(Thymus vulgaris) Labiatae

This well-loved plant is a perennial originating from the Mediterranean countries. There are numerous species, of different shapes and sizes, which gardeners delight in collecting; those most popular for the kitchen are the grey, shrubby garden thyme, and the green-leaved, refreshing lemon-scented thyme. Garden thyme has been used in many savoury and nourishing dishes for hundreds of years. With other good cooking herbs, it was hung in fragrant bunches to dry in the stillroom or kitchen, and when needed, the dry leaves would be rubbed off and used on their own, or mixed with sage and marjoram.

The warm smell of thyme brings to mind a tender chicken roasting in the oven, or perhaps a Christmas turkey, or a fat goose, especially if the thyme is freshly dried and still retains its typical piercing aroma. Thymol, an extract from the plant, is used in cough and digestive medicines.

Thyme tea is a popular beverage in some countries, and is quite delicious. Nicholas Culpeper, the early 17th century herbalist, says: "A strong infusion, drank as tea, is pleasant, and a very effectual remedy for head-ache, giddiness, and other disorders of that kind; and a certain remedy for that troublesome complaint, the night-mare."

There are certain dishes where a teaspoon or two of thyme alone is called for, and not a combination of herbs. It is used to flavour meat dishes, soups, bread stuffings, forcemeat, and some vegetables such as eggplant, mushrooms, onions, beetroot, zucchini and baby marrows.

Chicken · Mould

When the weather is hot and days are long and sunny, this smooth chicken mould is fragrant and cooling.

Simmer a chicken. Reserve the stock (about 3 cups). For the béchamel sauce, take 3 cups of chicken stock, melt 85 g (3 oz) butter in a saucepan, add 3 tablespoons plain flour, and blend; gradually pour in the stock with 1 cup milk added, stirring continuously. Put the béchamel on one side. Soften 2 envelopes gelatine in ½ cup hot water and stir until dissolved, then add to the béchamel sauce, mixing thoroughly. Add at once the following ingredients: 3 cups cooked chopped chicken, 2 tablespoons finely chopped shallot, 2 tablespoons chopped red capsicum, a little salt and pepper, ½ cup whipped cream, 1 tablespoon lemon juice, 1 teaspoon dried thyme, and ¼ teaspoon nutmeg. Chill until beginning to thicken, turn into a rinsed-out mould, and set in the refrigerator. Unmould onto a flat dish and surround with sprigs of thyme and cress.

Buttered · Marrow

Peel and slice thinly some fresh young marrows or zucchini. Place in a saucepan with 30 g (1 oz) butter, some salt and pepper, and 1 teaspoon dried thyme. Cover, and cook gently till soft. The vegetable must not be allowed to burn in the beginning; if necessary, add a little more butter. The flavour is so delicate that this may be served as an entrée or eaten between courses.

Turkey · Stuffing

This recipe for a stuffing for a 7 kg (15 lb) roast turkey was given to me by Mr and Mrs R. E. Allen, neighbours whose family have lived in the same district for 120 years. Their old stone house has high, cool ceilings, wide verandas and an old fireplace where a large black saucepan used to hang by a chain and hook.

Grate into a large bowl 8 cups soft breadcrumbs. Rub in 125 g (¼ lb) butter, add 1 onion (grated), 3 sticks celery (grated), 500 g (1 lb) raw pork (finely minced), the grated rind and juice of a lemon, 1 apple (grated), one 500 g tin crushed pineapple (drained), 2 eggs, ½ cup chopped parsley, 1 tablespoon dried thyme, and a little salt and pepper. Mix all ingredients together (the consistency should be crumbly). Before stuffing the bird, rub the cavity with garlic.

The pineapple juice may be mixed with the fat to baste the turkey.

Savoury · Meat · Balls
in · Sauce

Sauce: Simmer together for 15 minutes 900 ml (1½ pints) water, 1 onion, 1 bay leaf, a few black peppercorns, a pinch of salt, and 2 beef cubes. Remove the onion and bay leaf. The mixture is now ready for the meat balls (the sauce is thickened at a later stage).

Meat balls: Mix together 750 g (1½ lb) sausage mince or mince steak, 1 egg (beaten), 1 onion (finely chopped), 2 teaspoons dried thyme, and a little salt and pepper. With well-floured hands form the mixture into balls and drop them into the sauce. Simmer for 30 minutes. Remove the meat balls and keep them hot in a dish. Thicken the sauce with 1 dessertspoon cornflour blended with a little milk. Add chopped parsley, and pour this sauce over the meat balls. Serve hot.

· SPICES ·

Allspice

(Pimenta officinalis) Myrtaceae

Allspice comes from a tropical tree that is native to America and is also cultivated in the West Indies and Jamaica. The small sun-dried berries are sometimes known as pimento or Jamaica pepper, but are usually called allspice because the aroma and taste seem to be a combination of cinnamon, cloves, and nutmeg. Allspice is not a mixture of these three spices, as is sometimes thought.

Ground allspice is used in many spice blends and as a flavouring for various cakes, soups, meat dishes, milk puddings and vegetables. The berries are often tied in a muslin bag for use in the making of preserves, pickles, and chutney. Ground allspice with cinnamon helps to give pot-pourri its spicy fragrance.

Spiced · Veal · Roll

1 shoulder of veal, boned	1 dessertspoon chopped shallot
1 cup soft breadcrumbs	or onion
1 dessertspoon seeded raisins	Salt and pepper
Grated rind of an orange	4 tablespoons butter or
2 teaspoons mixed herbs	margarine
A few pieces of butter	1 teaspoon ground allspice
	Orange juice

Mix together the breadcrumbs, raisins, orange rind, herbs, pieces of butter, and shallot. Season with salt and pepper. Roll the meat up with this stuffing in the centre, tie with string, and rub the surface with butter and 1 teaspoon ground allspice. Put in a baking dish with 4 tablespoons fat (butter or margarine) and the juice from the grated orange. Bake in a moderate oven (175° to 190°C or 350° to 375°F), basting frequently. (If the liquid is reducing too much, add a little stock or water.) Allow 25 minutes to 500 g (1 lb) and 25 minutes over. If the liquid is too thin it may be thickened with a little flour, then poured over the veal, or served separately in a gravy boat.

Fried · Orange · Slices

Cut the pithy ends from oranges and discard. Slice the fruit into thin rounds and cover both sides with a mixture of sugar and ground allspice. Melt some butter or margarine and gently fry the orange slices in it, turning until the rinds are lightly browned. Serve hot with roast duck, rabbit, veal or pork.

Rose · Creams

Delicious with black coffee after dinner, this exquisite and rather exotic fondant brings a little of the Golden Road to Samarkand into the recipe collection: "... I will make her sweets like flowers. I will perfume my sweets with the perfume of roses, so that she shall say 'a rose'! and smell before she tastes...." (*Hassan*, by James Elroy Flecker).

250 g (½ lb) icing sugar	A few drops of rose water
1 teaspoon ground allspice	(obtainable from the
1 egg white	pharmacist)
	Red food colouring

Sift the icing sugar with the allspice. Beat the egg white slightly, and gradually add half the spiced icing sugar, beating well, then the rosewater and enough

colouring to make a rosy pink. Add the rest of the icing sugar, to make a stiff
consistency. Roll the fondant out on a flat board that has been sprinkled with icing
sugar. Cut into rounds with a small cutter and leave to harden.

Rose · Geranium · Jelly

This is a special preserve in the same mood as Rose Creams: delicately scented, ruby
coloured, and glistening, it may be put on the table with roast baby lamb, veal, or
poultry; or spread it on thin slices of bread-and-butter.

1 small bunch of rose geranium leaves	Juice of 2 small lemons, or 1 large lemon
5 cups sugar	4 cups water
1 teaspoon whole allspice	125 g (4 oz) powdered pectin
	Red food colouring

Wash the rose geranium leaves and steep them in the sugar, allspice, and lemon
juice for 1 hour. Place in a saucepan with the water and bring to the boil. Strain, add
the pectin, and boil again, stirring for about a minute. Add the food colouring. Pour
into small clean jars with a rose geranium leaf in each one. Seal the jars.

Cayenne

(Capsicum) Solanaceae

Cayenne pepper is the ground product from various species of dried
capsicum or red chili pepper. It is cultivated in the East Indies, Africa, and
many other parts of the world, in temperate as well as tropical zones. This is
an ornamental plant, bearing small, brilliant pods of vermilion fruit. An
excellent culinary spice, cayenne also has digestive properties.

Cayenne pepper is extremely hot and so it must be used sparingly. A
small amount is invaluable in cheese dishes, sauces, egg dishes, and with
shellfish. Cayenne is stimulating and zestful, and is a classic ingredient in a
Newburg Sauce.

Newburg · Sauce

3 tablespoons butter	2 cups thin cream or top milk
3 tablespoons plain flour	3 egg yolks, slightly beaten
1 teaspoon paprika	1 teaspoon sherry
A pinch of cayenne	Salt

Melt the butter in a saucepan. Blend in the flour, paprika, and cayenne. Add the cream gradually, stirring until the mixture thickens. Pour a little of this sauce onto the egg yolks, mix well, and return the mixture to the saucepan. Add sherry, and a pinch of salt. Carefully reheat, stirring constantly (do not boil). Add the cooked lobster pieces, prawns, or scallops, and heat them through. Transfer to a hot dish and serve immediately wtih steaming rice; or serve with triangles of hot buttered toast.

Cheese · Straws

125 g (¼ lb) butter	Cayenne
1 cup plain flour	Salt
3 tablespoons grated cheese	1 egg yolk

Rub the butter, flour, and cheese together, season with salt and add the egg yolk. If the mixture is too stiff, moisten with a little water. Roll out and cut into strips, forming three or four of them into circles. Bake in a hot oven (200°C or 400°F) for about 15 minutes. When the cheese straws are cool, slip them in bundles into the circles.

Egg · and · Potato · Pie

Peel and boil some potatoes and whip them until creamy with butter, milk, a little salt and pepper, and a grated onion. Spread thickly in a buttered ovenproof dish. Break an egg into a cup and slide it gently onto the potato; repeat, covering the potato with as many eggs as required. Mask the eggs with a little cream or top milk, and sprinkle with salt and cayenne. Bake in a medium-hot oven (190°C or 380°F) until the whites are set and the yolks are still soft-looking.

Tomato · Dumplings

125 g (4 oz) self-raising flour	1 dessertspoon chopped parsley
A walnut-sized piece of butter	(optional)
1 dessertspoon grated cheese	¼ teaspoon salt
6 tablespoons tomato juice	A pinch of cayenne

This is another delicious recipe from my neighbour Mrs R. E. Allen.

Sift the flour with the salt and cayenne, rub in the butter, add the cheese and, if liked, some chopped parsley. Stir in the tomato juice, making a very soft scone dough. Drop spoonfuls on top of a prepared favourite stew a little time before it is ready to serve (say 15 minutes)—putting the lid on and letting the dumplings cook gently for 12 to 15 minutes.

Chili Powder

Chili powder may be a mixture of dried ground chili peppers, aromatic seeds, spices, and herbs or it may be the ground peppers unmixed; the flavour differs with the manufacturers' formulas, and varies from mildly hot to very hot. The quantity of chili powder given in these recipes will vary with the brand you buy. At first it is better to use a little less than too much.

Cayenne, cumin, and oregano are often added in the preparation of the blend. The best and hottest chili powder comes from small bright red chilis known as bird's eye peppers. Originally this spice came from Mexico where the Aztecs introduced them to the conquering Spaniards in the sixteenth century.

The aroma of the powder is fiercely peppery, the colour being a rust red and the flavour hot and glowing. Its traditional use is in Chile con Carne, a

Mexican dish, but it has become indispensable in the making of certain sauces and in the blending of some curry powders.

When used prudently, chili powder sharpens the flavour of egg dishes, soups, and vegetables, and is particularly good as a flavouring in baked beans.

It once took me two days to prepare Boston Baked Beans for a barbecue, mixing triple quantities of haricot beans, salt pork, and molasses. The result was a sweet and sticky mess. A quick and easy dish using tinned baked beans and a sauce well spiced with chili powder has been an excellent standby since then. Here is the recipe.

Barbecue · Baked · Beans

Two 440 g tins baked beans
4 medium-sized to large
    tomatoes
2 onions
1 clove of garlic
1 tablespoon brown sugar

2 tablespoons butter or
    margarine
1 teaspoon mustard powder
1 dessertspoon chili powder
Salt

Pour boiling water onto the tomatoes, skin them, and chop coarsely. Peel and slice the onions and garlic and cook in the melted butter until soft. Add the brown sugar, mustard powder, chili powder, and some salt to taste. Cook until mushy (about 10 minutes), add the baked beans, and cook a little longer. Serves 8.

Chile · con · Carne

A fiery dish to take the place of curry for a change. Legend says that the Aztecs showed the *conquistadores* how to make it.

1 kg (2 lb) lean steak, chopped
    into cubes
Two 440 g tins red kidney
    beans
1 large tin tomatoes, or 3 cups
    tomato pieces
3 tablespoons vegetable oil
2 onions, peeled and chopped

2 cloves of garlic, chopped
2 teaspoons ground chili or less
    depending on strength
2 tablespoons plain flour
1 teaspoon oregano
1 teaspoon cumin seed
2 teaspoons salt

Heat the oil in an enamelled fireproof dish or a thick saucepan, add the onion and garlic, and cook until soft. Add the chili powder and meat, turning the meat until it is evenly browned. Blend in the flour, then add the tomato pieces (including liquid), oregano, and cumin. Cover, and simmer for 1 hour. Add the beans and salt, and cook for a further 15 minutes.

Chile con Carne (meaning chili with meat) is improved if made a day in advance: the spices will have truly permeated the meat, gravy, and beans. Serve hot with a crisp green salad and some icy-cold beer. For special occasions a wine from Alsace, Gewurztraminer, is suggested: its powerful bouquet is a fit companion for the hot Chile con Carne.

Mexican · Guacamole

The avocado pear, as well as chili powder, was once a favourite of the Aztecs.

Mash one ripe avocado pear until creamy, incorporate one small grated onion, one small, peeled, finely chopped tomato, a few drops of olive oil, and a pinch each of oregano, salt and chili powder. Place in a dish, with the stone of the avocado embedded in the mixture to prevent discoloration, and chill. Serve on a large lettuce leaf, as a savoury dip, with potato chips or plain biscuits.

Cinnamon

(Cinnamomum zeylanicum) Lauraceae

This spice, which comes from a tree native to Sri Lanka and Malabar, has been highly esteemed from remote times for its preservative and medicinal qualities, and as a flavouring for food and beverages.

When the trees are grown commercially the tender bark is peeled from the numerous long, slender shoots, and it curls into quills or sticks which are then dried in the sun. The fragrance of the bark comes from an essential oil, oil of cinnamon, which has valuable medicinal uses.

The dried bark from a cassia tree is also known as cinnamon, and is similar in flavour and appearance.

Cinnamon is used either whole or powdered. Ground cinnamon mixed with sugar on hot buttered toast is an old favourite; buttered tea cake strewn with sugar and cinnamon is always eaten down to the last delectable, spiced crumb. Ground cinnamon gives liveliness to milk puddings, mulled wines, chutneys, and cakes, and to various vegetables and stewed fruits. Combined with other spices it is a traditional ingredient in Christmas cakes, mince pies, and Christmas puddings, and is also one of the spices that go into the blending of curry powder.

Cinnamon sticks are used in a variety of ways: stirring black coffee with a piece of cinnamon gives it an Eastern aura, while on a bleak night a hot rum toddy flavoured with a little sugar and a twist of lemon peel and spiked with aromatic cinnamon sticks is most comforting, especially after a long journey.

In 1815 a tooth-powder was made by mixing "½ oz powdered cinnamon and ½ oz well-prepared chalk well together". This is one of the "receipts" in *Lotions and Potions*.

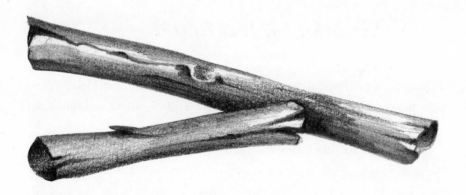

Treacle · Tart

As old-fashioned as caraway comfits and syllabubs, or pot-pourri and beeswax
candles, this delightful tart is as welcome today as it ever was—if one is fortunate
enough to come across it. A sprinkling of cinnamon over the top, although not
always traditional, is a pleasing addition. The pastry for this sweet is excellent when
made with fine wholemeal flour instead of refined white flour.

Short pastry
2 cups wholemeal flour
1 teaspoon baking powder
A pinch of salt
60 g (2 oz) butter or margarine
¼ cup cold water

Filling
3 tablespoons golden syrup
1 dessertspoon lemon juice
Grated lemon rind
3 tablespoons soft white breadcrumbs
1 teaspoon ground cinnamon

Sift the flour, baking powder and salt. Rub in the butter. Add enough
water to make a stiff dough. Roll out on a floured board. Line a greased flat
pie-plate with the pastry, pricking well all over.

For the filling, measure the syrup into a saucepan with a hot tablespoon
(this makes the measuring easier), add the lemon juice, grated rind, and
breadcrumbs. Warm slightly over low heat, pour into the pastry case,
sprinkle with the cinnamon, and bake in a moderate oven (175° to 190°C or
350° to 375°F) for 25 minutes. Serve cold with cream.

Devonshire · Junket

An old recipe from *Good English Food* by Florence White, this has been altered
slightly to suit ingredients available today.

Mix together in a bowl 1 tablespoon sugar, 1 tablespoon brandy or rum, ½
teaspoon ground cinnamon, and 2 crushed junket tablets. Pour onto these 600 ml
(1 pint) warm milk. Allow to set, then spread 150 ml (¼ pint) whipped cream over
the top and sprinkle with sugar. "When well made, junket should cut into smooth
shiny slices like jelly. Unlike jelly, it will set better and more quickly in a room of
ordinary temperature than a cold larder."

Flaming · Bananas

A lighted dessert is always exciting. This recipe is delicious as well.

Allow 2 bananas for each person. Peel and halve, place in a shallow fireproof dish, sprinkle with lemon juice, strew with sugar and cinnamon, and dot liberally with butter. Place under a medium-hot grill, and when soft and golden bring to the table and pour over 60 ml (2 fl oz) rum, and ignite it.

Sweet-sour · Brown · Beans

500 g (1 lb) brown
beans or haricot beans
1200 ml (2 pints) water
1/4 cup brown sugar
1/4 cup cider vinegar
1 tablespoon golden
syrup
2 teaspoons salt
A piece of cinnamon
stick

This is an excellent dish to serve with meat, or with crisp bacon for breakfast.

Wash the beans, cover with the water, and soak overnight. Do not change the water. Simmer next day for 30 minutes or until the beans are soft. Add the rest of the ingredients, and cook slowly with the lid off, stirring occasionally, for a further 30 minutes or until tender. Serve piping hot.

Rich · Spiced Christmas · Cake

1 3/4 cups plain flour
1/4 cup self-raising flour
250 g (1/2 lb) butter
1/2 cup raw sugar
1/2 cup best honey
5 eggs
1 level teaspoon of each of these:
salt, ground cinnamon,
ground cloves, ground
allspice, nutmeg
Juice and grated rind of 1
lemon
125 g (1/4 lb) of each of these:
glacé cherries, sultanas,
stoned raisins, crystallized
pineapple, glacé figs, mixed
peel, crystallized papaw,
shelled almonds
1 sherry glass of rum (or the
same amount of orange juice)

Prepare the fruit, halving the nuts and cherries and chopping the bigger fruit into small cubes. Sift the flours and spices together, and mix a small portion of this sifted spiced flour with the fruit. Cream the butter and sugar, add the honey, the eggs one at a time, and the lemon juice and grated rind. Fold in the sifted spiced flour, then the fruit, and lastly the rum or orange juice. Put into a 20 cm (8 inch) baking tin which has been lined with two thicknesses of brown paper (the inner layer oiled with butter). Bake in a slow oven (150°C or 300°F) for 3 to 4 hours. Weight when cooked is about 2 kg (4 lb).

Cloves

(Eugenia caryophyllata) Myrtaceae

Whole cloves are the dried flower-buds of an aromatic evergreen tree that is native to the Molucca Islands and is grown today in many hot countries. The pungent clove, either whole or ground, has become a necessary flavouring in a number of dishes. The volatile oil of cloves, a powerful antiseptic, is familiar to everyone.

The name clove is derived from the Latin word *clavus,* meaning nail, which the clove resembles in form.

A deliciously scented clove orange hung in the clothes closet was extremely popular a few centuries ago for repelling insects. (*Rosemary Hemphill's Herb Collection* describes the making of a clove orange.)

Held to the nostrils, a clove orange allayed the more offensive odours of the times. "It is not surprising that Cardinal Wolsey, when he ventured either into the lower regions of his own residence or risked the pervasive odours of the streets of London, commonly carried a spice-ball..." (*A Tudor Tragedy,* by Lacey Baldwin Smith).

Whole cloves are used as a flavouring in many kinds of preserves, mulled wines, stewed fruits, meat dishes, and soups. For stews or soups simmer with the other ingredients a whole onion studded with cloves and remove it before serving. Drop a clove into the hollowed-out centre of a cooking-apple, pack with butter and brown sugar, and bake in a moderate oven (175°C or 350°F) until tender.

When boiling fresh salt pork ("poor man's bacon") add to the water a few cloves, together with some peppercorns, a pinch of thyme, and a bay leaf. Simmer for about 2 hours, allow to cool in the water, drain, and keep chilled. The delicate texture of the pork permeated with the herbs and spices is often preferred to bacon.

A baked leg of ham, crumbed and studded with whole cloves and preserved pineapple, is a traditional favourite. A friend's large ham was treated in much the same way one Christmas Eve, with the effective and festive addition of red and green glacé cherries impaled on wooden picks—its tempting appearance resulted in our own ham being dealt with in a similar fashion immediately! The method is given in this chapter.

Clove-spiced hot pineapple cut in slices and eaten with barbecued meat or served with pork or ham is excellent: stud a carefully peeled pineapple with cloves and cook on a rotisserie (if you have one in your stove), or spike through the centre with a long skewer and turn slowly over the barbecue coals. Baste with melted butter and orange juice until well glazed and heated through.

Ground cloves are included in numerous recipes, such as fruit cake, buns mincemeat, milk puddings, and various sauces and vegetable dishes.

Festive · Ham

This recipe for garnishing a ham was given to me by a friend, Mrs R. R. Beck, whose ham I have described a little earlier in this chapter. The garnish may be applied either to cooked fresh ham or to tinned ham; it gives the meat an attractive, mouth-watering appearance and adds a delightful flavour.

If using a tinned ham, remove it carefully from the tin and put on a large plate or board. Remove every vestige of gelatine coating, and score the top deeply in a diamond pattern. With floured hands gently rub and pat flour all over the surface until it is quite dry, then stud the centre of each diamond with cloves.

Open a tin of pineapple rings, and drain them. Put the juice into a saucepan to heat, together with a generous portion of butter. (For the largest ham, 2 big tins of pineapple will be needed, and 250 g (½ lb) butter.)

Make a mixture of dry breadcrumbs, flour, brown sugar, and some dry mustard, add enough hot pineapple mixture to make a thick paste, and spread a portion all over the top and sides of the ham. Lift it into a baking dish lined with buttered foil, put into a hot oven (about 200°C or 400°F) and let it heat through for 10 to 15 minutes. Remove from the oven, and with a knife or spatula spread the remaining paste on the top and sides.

Spear red and green glacé cherries with wooden picks, putting one through each pineapple ring and onto the ham. Do this in a pleasing pattern around the sides first, then on the top, with the remaining cherries clustered together.

Return the ham to the oven for 20 minutes, allowing the coating to become crusty, then during the last 20 minutes baste frequently with the pineapple and butter, which must be kept bubbling on the stove. When all the liquid has been used, remove the ham from the oven and allow it to cool.

Apple · Pudding

This is essentially a family pudding; it is a simple recipe, and nourishing. The quantity given is quite large, so there should be enough for "seconds". Have plenty of cream on the table.

Peel, slice, and core enough cooking apples to thickly cover the bottom of a buttered baking dish; add 4 or 5 whole cloves and 2 tablespoons seedless raisins, sprinkle with lemon juice, and strew with sugar. Pour over this a batter made with 2 cups plain flour, a pinch of salt, ½ cup sugar, 2 eggs, and 600 ml (1 pint) milk. Bake in a moderate oven (175°C or 350°F) for 1 hour.

Beet · Bortsch

Make a good rich stock with 1 kg (2 lb) beef bones and a knuckle of veal covered with water, 1 medium-sized carrot, 1 parsnip, 2 tomatoes (chopped), salt, a little sugar, peppercorns, a bay leaf, thyme, and an onion stuck with cloves.

After it has simmered for 2 or 3 hours strain it through a colander and return it to the pot, adding 4 raw grated beetroot. Simmer for 10 minutes. The quantity should now be from 1800 to 2400 ml (3 to 4 pints).

In summer put the soup into a bowl in the refrigerator. If it does not jell overnight, dissolve gelatine in some hot water, stir into the soup, and chill. Serve jellied and icy cold with a spoonful of cream on each serving, and a dusting of ground cloves.

In winter omit the gelatine, add chopped frankfurts, and serve hot.

Vatroushki should be eaten with Bortsch: Tania, a friend of Russian extraction, has given her recipe, and having eaten these delicious little pies in her house I can warmly recommend them. They may accompany other vegetable soups or winter stews.

Vatroushki

Make your favourite short pastry, or the following: Sift together 60 g (2 oz) self-raising flour, 125 g (4 oz) plain flour, a pinch of salt, and 1 dessertspoon sugar. Rub in 125 g (4 oz) butter or margarine, add cold water, and mix to a stiff dough. Now mix together 250 g (½ lb) cream cheese, 1 egg, 1 tablespoon sugar, a pinch of salt, and 2 tablespoons plain flour. Roll the pastry fairly thinly and cut out circles with a teacup or large glass. Place a spoonful of filling in the centre of each pastry circle, and fold into envelopes, pinching to secure. Brush each with beaten white of egg and bake on a tray for about 20 minutes in a moderate oven (175° to 190°C or 350° to 375°F).

Curry Powder

The word "curry" immediately brings to mind spicy and colourful dishes from sun-drenched Eastern countries where "the dawn comes up like thunder" and on the air is the sound of "tinkly temple-bells".

In these countries, with their hot climates, a way of preparing food has been evolved that is suitable for the comfortable and healthy functioning of the body: it is said, for instance, that many of the hotter spices have a purifying effect on the intestines, and also that in humid, muggy weather curries help to "air-condition" the body.

Curry powder is not one spice but a blend of many spices which when combined with food gives it a unique flavour. In India each family grinds its own choice of aromatic seeds nearly every day. Flavours vary considerably from mild, medium, and sweet to very hot, all depending on which spices, and how many, are used in each blend. Instead of a powder, curry paste is sometimes preferred, in which case the prepared powder, perhaps with different spices and herbs added, is usually moistened with vinegar, pulverized garlic and vegetable oil, then cooked gently for a few minutes and sealed down.

Curry blends vary widely in different countries: Indonesian curry is fiercer as a rule than Indian curry, which to my mind, although hot, is extremely aromatic.

Chicken, rabbit, meat, fish, shellfish, vegetables, and hard-boiled eggs are any one of the main ingredients of a curry dish.

Indian · Curry

Accompaniments: Plenty of carefully cooked rice accompanies a curry, as well as relishes, which may number from three or four dishes to a great number. The traditional few are mango chutney, grated fresh coconut, or dried, desiccated coconut, shredded Bombay duck (which is a tasty cured fish), and Indian mint sauce, a refreshing and delicious combination of mint leaves and an onion minced together. Fresh coriander leaves are a popular garnish for a curry.

Curry powder: It is interesting to blend your own curry powder and to determine, yourself, the degree of heat and nuances of flavour. The recipe given here is intended to serve as a guide. Turmeric may be omitted and the same quantity of paprika used in its place, some people preferring the taste and colour. A little-known aromatic seed which is essential in the preparation of a curry blend is fenugreek. The small irregularly-shaped seeds are light golden-brown in colour, with a pleasantly bitter flavour and a warm, spicy scent.

An electric blender, grinding machine, or pestle-and-mortar may be used for the mixing and grinding of the powder and seeds. If desired, start from the beginning with the whole spice instead of the ground product: however, most spices bought already ground are simpler to use, and if the quality is good the result is satisfactory.

1 dessertspoon ground cinnamon	*1 tablespoon chili powder*
1 teaspoon ground cloves	*1 tablespoon ground coriander*
1 dessertspoon ground ginger	*1 tablespoon turmeric*
1 dessertspoon fenugreek seed	*1 dessertspoon cumin seed*
1 dessertspoon mustard seed	*2 teaspoons cardamom seed*

Grind and blend all ingredients together. Keep in an airtight jar. A few whole cloves may be added—they help to perfume the blend deliciously.

Meat · Curry

Ghee, which is clarified butter, is now available and is recommended as a shortening for the frying of the ingredients, although peanut oil may be used instead.

500 g (1 lb) trimmed beef or lamb, cut into cubes	*2 to 3 tomatoes, chopped*
3 tablespoons ghee or vegetable oil	*2 teaspoons salt*
	1 to 2 tablespoons curry powder
	2 tablespoons plain flour
1 onion, chopped	*150 ml (¼ pint) stock*
4 cloves of garlic, chopped	*1 tablespoon golden syrup*
1 apple, chopped	*30 g (1 oz) sultanas*
5 cm (2 inches) ginger root, peeled and sliced	*1 lemon, cut in half*

Heat the ghee or oil in a frying pan, and add the onion, garlic, apple, and ginger root. Fry gently until softened. Add the tomato, cook a little longer, then stir in the salt and curry powder. Fry for a few minutes. Transfer the contents of the frying pan to a heavy saucepan, add the meat and flour, and cook till brown. Gradually pour in the stock, then stir in the golden syrup, together with the sultanas and lemon halves. Turn the heat very low, put a lid on the saucepan, and simmer for 2 hours, stirring occasionally. About 15 minutes before serving, pick up the lemon halves with the kitchen tongs and squeeze them so that the juice goes into the curry (discard the lemon halves when this has been done). Serve with rice and accompaniments.

Indonesian · Curry

Accompaniments: With this curry serve the rice individually moulded for each person. Press the cooked rice into cups and then unmould immediately. (The rice may be kept hot by standing the cups in a covered shallow pan of gently boiling water before unmoulding it.) As many side dishes as you wish may be prepared, as long as they include prawn crisps, fried bananas, hot chutney, and very small meat balls.

Coconut milk: The liquid used in Indonesian curry is coconut milk, which is not the milk from the inside of this nut but an infusion of grated coconut and water. It is made by pouring hot water onto desiccated coconut, the quantities usually being 3 tablespoons of coconut to 1 cup of water. After the coconut has been soaking for 1 hour or more, strain the liquid through a muslin cloth and gently squeeze the residue through the cloth to extract the goodness and flavour. A lesser quantity of grated fresh coconut to the same amount of water may be used instead.

Hot · Chicken · Curry

Substitute fish or meat for the chicken in this recipe if you wish. This dish improves with keeping and should be made the day before it is to be eaten.

1 small chicken, disjointed and cut up
2 tablespoons peanut oil
1 onion, chopped
2 cloves of garlic, chopped
2 tablespoons peanut butter
2 teaspoons salt
600 ml (1 pint) coconut milk (see preceding recipe)

Spice mixture

1 teaspoon ground chili or less depending on strength
1 dessertspoon ground cumin
1 dessertspoon turmeric
1 dessertspoon ground coriander
1 dessertspoon ground ginger
2 lemon or lime leaves

Warm the oil in a saucepan, and fry the onion and garlic in it until soft. Add the peanut butter and the salt. Mix the spices together in a small dish and add 2 or 3 tablespoons of them to the mixture in the saucepan. Add the flour. Stir and cook until well blended. Gradually pour in the coconut milk, stirring all the time. Add the chicken, then the lemon leaves, and simmer for 2 hours. Serve with rice and accompaniments.

Papaw · Pickle

From Mathild's *Island Recipe Book*, compiled in the New Hebrides by the women living there, comes this curry-flavoured papaw pickle.

Cut 500 g (1 lb) green tomatoes into small pieces, sprinkle well with salt, and leave overnight. Next day, cut into small pieces a small, very green papaw (first removing the seeds), 3 cucumbers, 2 onions, and 9 small chilis. Mix with the tomato, adding 5 teaspoons of brown sugar and 4 teaspoons of good curry powder. Cover with vinegar and boil till soft. Bottle.

Ginger

(Zingiber officinale) Zingiberaceae

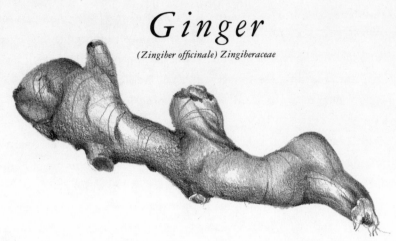

Ginger is a native of tropical Asia, grown also in Africa, India, China, and Jamaica. The perennial root is tuberous and creeping; after the plant has died down, the root is dried and then preserved in syrup, or it is crystallized or ground.

Ginger is an important ingredient in the blending of curry powder, and its rich, clean tang has been appreciated for hundreds of years in many different kinds of food. Whole pieces in syrup sealed in pretty blue-and-white or other attractively coloured patterned jars from the Orient have been a favourite of mine since childhood. In its crystallized, sugary form ginger makes a pungent sweetmeat, and small pieces added to the ingredients give added flavour to rich spice cakes.

Green ginger is sometimes called for in recipes: this is usually available canned and preserved in liquid. Pieces of the whole root are used in marinades for teriyaki (a recipe for Beef Teriyaki is given in this section), in pickles and chutney, in Chinese food, and in some recipes for ginger beer and ginger wine. Ground ginger may nearly always be substituted for the whole root if necessary, and in this form it is used in ginger beer, ginger snaps, gingerbread, sauces, spice cakes, preserves, and sweets, and to flavour certain meat and vegetable dishes.

Every household has its favourite spices and its favourite containers for them. We still have a silver pepper shaker with ginger in it which belonged to my grandfather. Sometimes we take it out of the cabinet and shake it over apple pie, just as he did. The ginger still has a bite and mellowness about it, and happy moments are re-lived as the gleaming little container is passed round the table.

Gingerbread men and other gingerbread fancies were sold at country fairs in England in olden days. Flora Thompson gives us a glimpse of high-days and holidays of the past in her *Lark Rise to Candleford*. Of one feast-day holiday she writes: "The women made their houses very clean and neat for Feast Monday, and, with hollyhocks nodding in at the open windows and a sight of the clean, yellow stubble of the cleared fields beyond, and the hum of friendly talk and laughter within, the tea parties were very pleasant. At the beginning of the 'eighties the outside world remembered Fordlow Feast to the extent of sending one old woman with a gingerbread stall. On it were gingerbread babies with currants for eyes...."

Mango · Mousse

The incomparable taste of mangoes is enhanced by the ginger in this sweet with a tropical fragrance.

2 large ripe mangoes	*1 envelope gelatine (dissolved in*
1 cup water	*¼ cup hot water)*
½ cup sugar	*2 eggs, separated*
1 teaspoon ground ginger	*300 ml (½ pint) cream,*
	whipped

Simmer the water, sugar, and ginger together for a few minutes. Peel and slice the mangoes, add to the syrup, and poach until soft. Sieve them (syrup included) or put into a blender. Add the dissolved gelatine and return the mixture to the saucepan with the egg yolks. Stir over low heat until smooth and thickened (do not boil). Remove from the stove, cool slightly, and fold in the whipped cream and the beaten egg whites. Pour into a bowl or into individual dishes. Chill. Just before serving, cover the top with shredded coconut (for extra flavour and crispness brown the coconut beforehand in the oven).

Red · Tomato · Relish

A quick, uncomplicated recipe when tomatoes are plentiful. The ground ginger and chili powder give an invigorating flavour to this relish.

3 kg (6 lb) red tomatoes
2 onions
2 cloves of garlic
500 g (1 lb) raw or brown
  sugar
1 cup herb or cider vinegar

60 g (2 oz) common salt
2 teaspoons ground ginger
1 teaspoon ground mace
1 teaspoon ground chili or less
  depending on strength
1 dessertspoon dried oregano

Thickening

2 tablespoons plain flour and some vinegar

Pour some boiling water onto the tomatoes and leave for a few minutes. Drain the water off. Peel and chop the tomatoes. Peel and slice the onions and garlic. Put all ingredients except the thickening together into a saucepan and boil gently for 30 minutes. Blend the flour with enough vinegar to make a thin paste, pour into the mixture, and boil for a further 15 minutes, stirring all the time. Cool, then seal the relish in jars.

Beef · Teriyaki

The steak in this recipe may be replaced by pork, veal, or chicken.

750 g (1½ lb) rump steak,
  cut into chunky cubes
1 medium-sized tin pineapple
  rings, cut into quarters

1 small jar stuffed olives
Red glacé cherries

Marinade

1 clove garlic, crushed
¼ cup soy sauce
1 teaspoon ground ginger

1 tablespoon sherry
Juice from pineapple rings

Combine the ingredients for the marinade. Add the steak, leaving it to soak for 1 hour. Now thread alternately on 15 cm (6 inch) metal skewers the meat, pineapple pieces, olives, and cherries. Grill, turning frequently and basting with the marinade. Allow 2 or 3 skewers for each person. Serve with boiled rice and a green salad.

For a barbecue, increase the quantities and thread on very long skewers, adding some or all of the following: mushrooms, small onions or pickled onions, capsicum slices, stoned prunes, thickly sliced dill cucumbers, gherkins, wedges of tomato, and some stoned black olives. Rest the skewers over the coals, turning them until the food is cooked.

Mace and Nutmeg

(Myristica fragrans) Myristicaceae

Mace and nutmeg are grouped together because they both come from the same thirty-foot tropical tree, which grows in the Molucca Islands, Sri Lanka, Sumatra, and Malaya. In some countries the species are different, and accordingly the shape and flavour of the fruit varies.

Imagine a section of the fruit cut in half: first there is the outer covering or shell, then the scarlet network or aril, which when dried is known as mace; within this lacy covering is the nutmeg.

The flavours of mace and nutmeg are very similar, mace being more piercingly aromatic. If mace is difficult to obtain, nutmeg may be substituted.

Nutmeg

Nutmeg usually comes to us ground, but the hard, dried seed may be kept in a small jar and grated when required. In former days every household had its nutmeg grater and its whole nutmegs. This spice has a pleasing and rather crisp, dry quality, and is often included in rich food. An egg flip or eggnog is not complete without a sprinkling of nutmeg on the top: besides having an agreeable flavour, nutmeg is supposed to have a soothing effect on the digestive system. It is interesting to read that its use in medicine is "as a stimulant and carminative". (A carminative is a medicine to cure colic or flatulence.) The flavour of nutmeg does not dominate when mixed with other herbs and spices.

Ground or freshly grated nutmeg flavours milk puddings, cakes, biscuits, soups, breads, oyster and fish dishes, pumpkin pie, cream sauces, some meat dishes, and nearly all beverages made with milk.

Mace

Mace may be obtained ground or whole. When whole it is known as a "blade" of mace. The colour of dried mace is more golden than that of nutmeg, and the flavour is stronger, therefore a smaller quantity is required in cooking. Mace in a Sauce Suprême for fish is excellent. It is often called for in pickle and chutney recipes, in cheese dishes, to give character to creamed spinach, steamed young carrots, and mashed potato. Grilled, buttered trout may be lightly sprinkled with salt, freshly ground pepper, and a dusting of mace, all that this delicately flavoured fish needs.

Fish · Suprême

This dish may be made the day before and kept in the refrigerator, removing it an hour before it is ready to go in the oven.

Cover 1 kg (2 lb) raw fish (leatherjacket or your favourite fish) with water, add a little salt and a bay leaf, and simmer until the fish is cooked. Drain, reserving the liquid. Flake the fish while it is still hot, removing all bones, and put into an oven-proof dish.

Make Sauce Suprême as follows: Melt 125 g (¼ lb) butter or margarine, blend in ½ cup plain flour, and gradually add 900 ml (1½ pints) fish stock, stirring constantly until it thickens. Combine 4 eggs, 150 ml (¼ pint) thick cream, 2 tablespoons white wine, ½ teaspoon ground mace (or 1 teaspoon ground nutmeg) in a bowl, pour in some of the hot mixture, season with salt and pepper, mix well, then return all to the remaining contents of the saucepan. Stir gently over low heat for a moment only.

Pour the sauce over the fish, and top with soft white breadcrumbs which have been tossed in melted butter. Bake in a slow oven (about 150°C or 300°F) until heated through. Serve hot with rice and chilled white wine.

Savoury · Welsh · Rarebit

3 tablespoons butter or margarine	2 teaspoons beef extract (mixed into ½ cup hot water)
4 tablespoons plain flour	250 g (½ lb) grated Cheddar cheese
1 teaspoon mustard	Salt and pepper
1 cup milk	Ground nutmeg

This cheese rarebit goes a long way.

Melt the butter, stir in the flour and mustard, slowly pour the milk in, then add the diluted beef extract. Add the cheese, season with salt and pepper, and cook, stirring until the mixture is smooth. Serve hot on buttered toast, topped with nutmeg.

Avocado · Soup

The most ambrosial soup I know. Ground or grated nutmeg sprinkled on each serving helps to minimize the richness without spoiling the bland texture.

900 ml (1½ pints) chicken broth (may be made with cubes)
2 large ripe avocado pears

300 ml (½ pint) cream
Extra cream
Ground nutmeg
Salt and pepper

Peel and stone the avocados, mash them, and put them into the chicken broth. Heat, then stir in 300 ml (½ pint) cream. Put the mixture through a sieve to remove any lumps, then return it to the saucepan, adding salt and pepper to taste. Bring slowly to simmering point without allowing it to boil. Serve hot with a dessertspoon of cream and a sprinkling of nutmeg in each bowl.

Mulled · Ale

This recipe is from *Mrs Beeton's Book of Household Management*.

1200 ml (1 quart) good ale
1 glass rum or brandy
1 tablespoon castor sugar
A pinch of ground cloves

A pinch of grated nutmeg
A good pinch of ground ginger

Put the ale, sugar, cloves, nutmeg, and ginger into an ale warmer or stewpan, and bring nearly to boiling point. Add the brandy, and more sugar and flavouring if necessary, and serve at once.

Paprika

(Capsicum annuum) Solanaceae

Paprika comes from a red, sweet pepper that is native to Central America and cultivated today in different parts of Europe and the United States. It is dried, ground, and sometimes blended with other peppers of the same family that differ in degrees of pungency. The best paprika is now said to come from Hungary.

The colour of paprika should be a rich, bright red, and the aroma warm and sweet. A splendid spice to use for flavouring, it is quite often regarded as a garnish only. Paprika gives Hungarian goulash its characteristic colour and taste; it is also valuable as a flavouring for delicately textured food such as crab, fish, chicken, cream sauces, eggs, and cheese dishes. It may be mixed into rice dishes and shaken onto split, baked potatoes, hors d'œuvre, crumbed casseroles, or salads.

Waldorf · Salad

Paprika gives sparkle and relish to this salad, which is crisp with celery, apples, and nuts, glistens with orange cubes, and is folded together with a creamy sauce. It makes a pleasant change from a tossed green salad to serve with a main course.

1 crisp eating apple, chopped
1 cup diced celery
1 large sweet orange, peeled and chopped
1 packet shelled, halved walnuts
Paprika

Sauce

1 cup cream
1 tablespoon lemon juice
1 tablespoon sugar
1/2 teaspoon dry mustard
Salt and pepper

To make the sauce, stir the lemon juice, sugar, and mustard, with a little salt and pepper, into the cream, and beat till thick. Mix together the apple, celery, orange, and nuts and pour the sauce over. Toss well, then chill in the refrigerator. When ready to serve, turn onto a bed of lettuce, or onto leaves of fresh herbs, and sprinkle rosily with the paprika.

Ten · Minute · Crab · Paprika

This is an excellent entrée and makes a pleasant snack for a late supper.

Open a tin of crabmeat and flake it, removing all the sharp pieces. Have ready 600 ml (1 pint) of rich white sauce. Heat (do not boil), stirring in an egg which has been beaten with 1 dessertspoon paprika. In a separate saucepan warm 2 tablespoons brandy, set alight and carefully add to the sauce. Stir well, then add the crab. Pour into a buttered ovenproof dish or buttered scallop-shells, and top with breadcrumbs which have been tossed in melted butter. Brown in the oven. Serve with thin slices of lemon and very small squares of brown bread-and-butter.

Hungarian · Veal · Goulash

1 kg (2 lb) veal steak	1 bay leaf
2 onions, sliced	1 dessertspoon lemon juice
1 tablespoon shortening	1 cup cream
1 tablespoon paprika	1 tablespoon plain flour
1 cup stock (may be made with	Salt and pepper
a beef cube)	

Cut the veal into 5 cm (2 inch) cubes. Soften the onion in the shortening, add the meat, and brown all over. Add the paprika, and salt and pepper to taste, and cook a little longer. Add the stock, put in the bay leaf, cover the saucepan, and simmer for 1 hour, stirring occasionally. (Add a little more liquid if becoming too dry.) Pour the lemon juice into the cream, blend in the flour, add to the veal, and stir until thickened. Serve hot with poppy-seed noodles (page 103).

Pepper

(Piper nigrum) Piperaceae

Black pepper and white pepper are both produced from the same climbing vine, which is native to the East Indies and cultivated in India, Sumatra, and Java. Pepper has been a valued spice for many hundreds of years; in the Middle Ages it was prized nearly as highly as gold and silver.

For black pepper, the berries are first picked from the vine, and then dried, when they become dark in colour, wrinkled, and very hot.

For white pepper, which is the same fruit, the dark outer husk is removed, leaving the smooth, parchment-coloured core, milder in flavour than black pepper.

Both black pepper and white pepper come in several forms: ground to a powder, left whole, or sometimes coarsely ground and mixed with sweet red pepper, sugar, and spices to make a delicious seasoned pepper. It is interesting to make your own mixture: over a small dish grind black and white pepper together in a mill, into the powder put a little sugar, ground cinnamon, paprika, and a pinch of ginger. Use this as a garnish as well as for flavouring.

Whole pepper, or peppercorns, are becoming increasingly popular: they may be poured into a mill and freshly ground over food while it is being prepared, and the mill may be passed round at table as well. The flavour of newly ground pepper is more aromatic, and it is a matter of taste whether black or white pepper is used for this purpose. Sometimes a mixture of the two is preferred.

A few whole peppercorns should be dropped into soups, stews, and casseroles, or when boiling salted pork, mutton, or beef. They are used too when making pickles, spice vinegars, and sauces.

Pickled · Onions

One year a crop of white onions failed and we were given a quantity of pearly little vegetables that were too small to send to market. When pickled they were crisp and spicy. Here is the way to pickle them: Peel 1 kg (2 lb) of small white onions, strew 30 g (1 oz) salt over them, and leave overnight. Next day, boil 1200 ml (1 quart) of cider vinegar with 1 dessertspoon each of black peppercorns and whole cloves for 10 minutes. Wash the salt off the onions, shake dry in a colander, and add to the vinegar. Boil for 5 minutes. Remove the onions and pack into small jars or a large pickle jar, then pour the vinegar onto them. Seal the jars when the contents are cold.

Spiced · Vinegar

Empty 1 bottle of white wine or cider vinegar into a saucepan. Add 1 teaspoon each of peppercorns, whole cloves, ground ginger, and celery seed, also 1 cinnamon stick, 1 dried chili, and 1 dessertspoon sugar. Bring to the boil and simmer for 3 minutes. Cool and bottle without straining.

Sausages · and · Lentils

1 kg (2 lb) beef sausages	½ teaspoon peppercorns
2 medium-sized onions	2 tablespoons red lentils
1 clove of garlic	Salt
3 cloves	Plain flour
1 bay leaf	

Roll the sausages in plain flour, and peel and slice the onions and garlic. Put the ingredients in layers in an ovenproof dish and cover with water. With the lid on, bake in a slow oven (130° to 150°C or 275° to 300°F) for 2½ hours.

Saffron

(Crocus sativus) Iridaceae

Saffron comes from the orange-coloured stigmas of a mauve-flowering crocus, native to Asia and parts of Europe. It is a rare and expensive spice because only the hand-picked stigmas are used and it requires over 200,000 of these to make one pound: fortunately only a small quantity is needed to colour and flavour food.

Saffron has been prized from the most ancient times for use in food, medicine, and dyes; in *The Bible as History* we are told that the colourful garments of the Children of Israel owed their brightness to nature: saffron for yellow, madder-root for red, and the murex snail supplied purple.

Culpeper describes saffron as being a herb of the sun, and says: "It refreshes the spirits, and is good against fainting-fits and the palpitation of the heart." But he cautions against an immoderate amount being taken. Sir Francis Bacon thought so highly of this herb that he said: "What made the English people sprightly was the liberal use of saffron in their broths and sweet-meats." (Eleanour Sinclair Rohde, *A Garden of Herbs.*) In medieval days saffron was also popular as a dye for the hair.

There is a town in England called Saffron Walden where this crocus was grown extensively; the arms of the town have three saffron flowers pictured within turreted walls. Saffron Hill, now a London thoroughfare, was once part of the gardens of Ely Place where quantities of saffron were grown.

The warmly bitter aroma and the gold colour of saffron give certain dishes their traditional flavour and colour: the saffron cakes of Cornwall are well known; saffron is an important ingredient in the classic French fish soup Bouillabaisse, in Arroz con Pollo (Rice with Chicken), and in Paella; it also enhances some sauces, breads, cakes, fish, chicken, and rice dishes.

Today saffron comes from different parts of the world and is almost as precious as gold dust; when ground to a russet powder it is packaged carefully in envelopes; it is also available in whole orange and gold threads. When using the threads, crush the required number and infuse in the hot milk or other liquid which the recipe calls for. The powder may be infused in liquid or sifted with flour.

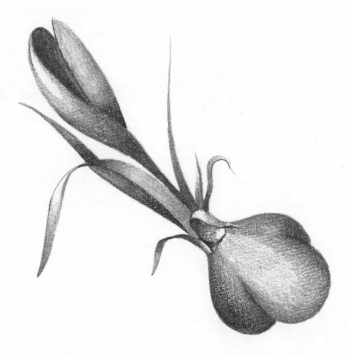

Saffron · Gooseberry · Shortcake

2 cups self-raising flour
1/4 teaspoon powdered saffron
1/4 teaspoon salt
1/2 cup brown sugar
125 g (1/4 lb) butter or
  margarine

2 eggs, beaten
1/2 cup milk
One 500 g tin gooseberries
1 dessertspoon arrowroot,
  blended with a little milk

This is a refreshing sweet in summer. It may be eaten for afternoon tea if you wish.

Sift the flour, saffron, and salt into a bowl, add the brown sugar, rub in the butter, and add the eggs and milk. Spoon into a greased, lightly floured 20 cm (8 inch) recessed tin and bake in a hot oven (200°C or 400°F) for 15 minutes. Cool and turn onto a cake rack. Open the tin of gooseberries, drain the liquid into a saucepan and simmer it until it is reduced a little. Thicken it with the blended arrowroot, stir in the gooseberries, cool, and pour onto the shortcake. Serve with thick cream.

If fresh gooseberries are used, stew the fruit in the usual way, thickening the syrup with arrowroot when cooked.

Bouillabaisse

It is said that only in France may one taste real bouillabaisse, for the original recipe calls for several different kinds of fish that are not available in other countries. Nevertheless, there are many versions of this popular fish soup, and this one has a delicious and unusual flavour and aroma, is quite inexpensive, and is quickly prepared even by the busiest cook.

2 kg (4 lb) boned, filleted fish
  cut into pieces
1/2 cup vegetable oil
4 tomatoes, peeled and chopped
3 onions, peeled and chopped

2 cloves of garlic, cut very fine
1 teaspoon saffron
1 wine-glass white wine
1/2 teaspoon thyme
Freshly ground pepper
1 teaspoon salt

Trout is excellent if available.

Heat the oil in a large casserole, and fry in it the tomato, onion, garlic, and saffron, together with salt and pepper. Add the sliced fish, wine, thyme, and bay leaf, cover with water (about 2400 ml or 2 quarts), bring to the boil, and simmer for 10 minutes. Serve hot. Accompany with slices of a French loaf.

Saffron · Risotto

A delicately flavoured golden dish to serve with fricasseed chicken, fish, or a veal casserole. This method of cooking a risotto is recommended provided the cooking time is watched and the quantities given are measured accurately.

60 g (2 oz) butter
1 medium-sized onion, chopped
1 clove of garlic, chopped
1 small green capsicum,
    chopped

1 cup rice
1 pint chicken broth (may be
    made with chicken cubes)
¼ teaspoon saffron

Infuse the saffron, whether ground or whole, in the hot chicken broth. Melt the butter in a fireproof pan or casserole, add the onion, garlic, and capsicum, then the rice, turning until the grains are shining and coated. Add the saffron-flavoured chicken broth. Bring to the boil, put the lid on, and place in a moderate oven (175°C or 350°F) to bake for 30 minutes.

Sunny · Saffron · Dumplings

1 cup self-raising flour
A pinch of salt
60 g (2 oz) butter

2 teaspoons dried parsley
¼ cup milk
A pinch of powdered saffron

These dumplings are for a meat or chicken casserole.

Sift the flour and salt into a bowl, rub in the butter, and add the parsley. Heat the milk and saffron together, add to the flour, and mix to a firm dough. Pat out on a floured surface, and roll lightly. Mark deep incisions in the form of squares with a knife, slide in one piece onto the cooked, bubbling casserole, replace the lid, and cook for 20 minutes. Serve immediately.

Saffron · Buns

This is an old recipe from an authority on English folk cookery, Florence White, who includes it in her collection, *Good English Food*.

Take 3½ lb (1750 g) flour, ½ lb (250 g) butter, ½ pint (300 ml) cream of milk; set the milk on the fire, put in the butter and a good deal of sugar, strain saffron to your taste into the milk, take three or four eggs, with one yolk and one ounce (30 g) of compressed yeast, put the milk to it when almost cold, with salt, and coriander seeds; knead them all together, make them up into small cakes, or buns, set them to rise and bake them in a quick oven.

To prepare the saffron take half a drachm (17 mg) and cut very fine with scissors, pour over half a cup of boiling water and steep overnight.

Salt

Salt is included here because it is essential in all types of cooking. Its value as an antiseptic and its use in medicine are well known.

Salt, or sodium chloride, occurs naturally in sea water; mineral deposits of rock salt are the crystalline evidence of vast salt lakes and seas long since vanished from the earth's surface. Smaller quantities are found near hot springs and mineral waters, the salt from the solution being precipitated and occurring in layers.

Refined free-running table salt (which has magnesium carbonate added to prevent it from caking) is seen on every grocer's shelf, as well as a coarser quality known as common salt. Salt crystals for grinding over food should be put into a wooden salt mill as a companion to the pepper mill. The crystals are obtainable from some butchers' shops and delicatessens.

There are many seasoned salts which have gone through a process to capture the flavour required; some popular flavours at present are celery salt, garlic salt, mushroom salt, parsley salt, salt seasoned with spices and herbs, and health salt containing dehydrated vegetables and herbs. There is a hickory-smoked salt smelling of wood smoke, which is particularly attractive to people living in the depths of big cities miles from forests and open country.

A seasoned salt for the kitchen, barbecues, or the table is very useful: an interesting blend is easily made by a selection from the spice shelf. A pestle-and-mortar for grinding and pounding the ingredients together is needed, and whether it is made from marble or smooth wood it is a practical and handsome kitchen implement.

Seasoned · Salt

Grind together in a mortar 1 teaspoon celery seed and 1 teaspoon dried rosemary. Add 1 teaspoon each of ground mace and paprika, ½ teaspoon sugar, and 1 table-spoon table salt. Put in a small airtight bottle and use as required.

Monosodium · Glutamate

Monosodium glutamate, or MSG, is mentioned as an ingredient in many recipes. Its purpose is to enhance and bring out, or to restore, the characteristic flavour of food, not to impart an aroma of its own. Ideally it is made from crystals produced from vegetable protein, and has various trade names, its description being "essence of taste". MSG derived from chemicals is not recommended at all.

Turmeric

(Curcuma longa) Zingiberaceae

Turmeric is a perennial plant of the ginger family, native to India and parts of Asia. The dried, aromatic root is ground to a brilliant yellow powder which gives a commercial curry blend its typical colour and much of its flavour; it is used in the East as a dye for cottons and silks as well as for flavouring food.

The vivid hue and pungent scent of this spice seems essentially Eastern in character: "What is the scent of a Bazaar? Who can say?...Taking it as a whole, however, I fancy the smell of turmeric brings back more than anything else the wonderful kaleidoscope of colours in an Indian bazaar." (*India,* by Mortimer Menpes.)

The mellow fragrance and bright colour of turmeric has made it popular as an ingredient in pickles and chutneys, and in mustard-powder blends. A small amount may be used for colouring cakes, and it is excellent in rice dishes; turmeric is often added to fish kedgeree, devilled eggs, French dressings, and fish stews; a pinch stirred into a smooth white sauce gives colour and an elusive, rather peppery, taste.

Kedgeree

This is a good luncheon or breakfast dish, which may be prepared the night before it
is needed.

1 cup cooked rice
500 g (1 lb) any one of the
    following: smoked and
    flaked cooked cod, tinned
    salmon or tuna, prawns or
    lobster
125 g (¼ lb) butter or
    margarine
1 onion, peeled and chopped

1 capsicum, chopped
2 cloves of garlic, chopped
2 teaspoons turmeric
Juice of a lemon
½ teaspoon ground ginger
Salt and pepper
2 hard-boiled eggs, shelled
1 teaspoon dried parsley

Melt butter and soften onion, capsicum, and garlic in it. Add turmeric, lemon
juice, ginger, and a little salt and pepper. Lightly stir in fish and rice, and when
thoroughly mixed together turn into a dish and heat in the oven before serving.
Garnish with eggs cut into circles, and with parsley.

Tropical · Potato · Salad

3 cups diced cooked potatoes
1 cup banana circles
1 cup finely chopped shallots
    (include the green part)

A little lemon juice
2 teaspoons turmeric
1 cup mayonnaise
2 hard-boiled eggs, sliced
Salt and pepper

This salad has a pleasant and subtle combination of flavours.

Sprinkle lemon juice over the banana circles to prevent discoloration. While the
potatoes are still warm, season them with salt and pepper and add the banana and
shallot. Blend the turmeric with the mayonnaise and mix gently through the salad.
Add the egg slices last. Chill before serving.

French · Dressing

Take 1 tablespoon of lemon juice or white vinegar and blend in 2 tablespoons of
vegetable oil, some freshly ground pepper, a little salt, a pinch of sugar, and a few
grains of mustard powder. Prepare well in advance and keep in a small screw-top jar
or covered jug until the last moment, before the salad is tossed, when the mixture
should be thoroughly stirred or vigorously shaken.

This dressing is also used as a marinade. One teaspoon of turmeric added to the
mixture with the mustard is delicious, either when tossing a salad or for marinades.

AROMATIC SEEDS

Aniseed

(Pimpinella anisum) Umbelliferae

Anise is a sun-loving annual plant, native to Middle Eastern countries. The clusters of white flowers are followed by small oval seeds which are light brown in colour and taste warmly of licorice. Anise was known many thousands of years ago: it is referred to in the Bible and, as I mentioned at the beginning of this book, the Romans ate cakes made with these digestion-aiding seeds to conclude their enormous feasts. Helen Noyes Webster quotes from Grieve and Leyel: "It was used in a spiced cake at the end of a meal by

the Romans in Virgil's time to prevent indigestion; a cake which was brought in at the end of a marriage feast, it is perhaps the origin of today's spicy wedding cake."

Anise is used extensively in cooking, in medicine for digestive complaints, and as an ingredient in the liqueur Anisette. It is grown mainly for the seeds, although the leaves may be used in salads and as a garnish. Aniseed flavours breads, rolls, cakes, biscuits, and sweet pastry for fruit pies and tarts. It may also be used in cheeses, in milk beverages and puddings, and when cooking vegetables such as carrots and cabbage, when little or no water is used.

With some of the other fragrant seeds, aniseed may be pressed into butter to be spread on top of "brown-and-serve" rolls before they are put into the oven. Line a rustic basket with a table napkin and fill it with hot rolls, some topped with aniseed, others with sesame seed, poppy seed, dill seed, celery seed, or caraway seed. If you have herbs growing, garnish with leaves of anise, burnet, or dill. These rolls are excellent to serve with a main dish for luncheon or supper, the seeds giving them a delicious flavour and crunchiness.

Anise · Cookies

125 g (4 oz) butter or margarine
1 cup raw sugar
1 egg
125 g (4 oz) self-raising flour

A pinch of salt
1 cup rolled oats
1½ cups desiccated coconut
2 teaspoons aniseed

Cream the butter and sugar, add the egg and beat well. Stir in the sifted flour and salt, and add the rolled oats, coconut, and aniseed, mixing well together to a stiff consistency. Roll into small balls between the hands, put on a greased oven tray, and bake in a moderate oven (175° to 190°C or 350° to 375°F) for 12 to 15 minutes. Cool on the tray before storing.

Red · Cabbage · Casserole · with · Pork Sausages

Aniseed gives its quota to the other delicious smells which help to make this a fragrant winter dish for six hungry people. Serve it at supper-time with baked jacket potatoes, and with mulled ale.

1 red cabbage	150 ml (1/4 pint) strong
3 onions, peeled and chopped	chicken stock (made with 1
3 green apples, chopped with	cube)
the skin on	1 teaspoon black peppercorns
3 tablespoons raw or brown	1/2 teaspoon salt
sugar	1 dessertspoon aniseed
2 tablespoons cider vinegar	1 kg (2 lb) pork sausages
	250 g (1/2 lb) bacon

Shred the cabbage and put it into a large casserole with the onion, apple, sugar, vinegar, chicken stock, peppercorns, salt, and aniseed. Mix well, put the lid on, and bake in a slow oven (150°C or 300°F) for 3 hours, putting scrubbed potatoes into the oven for the last 1½ hours. Towards the end of the cooking time, fry the sausages and bacon, turning them until browned and cooked. Put them into the cabbage mixture before serving with the baked potatoes.

Aniseed · Carrots

Cut carrots into straws, put them in a saucepan with 2 tablespoons water, 1 tablespoon raw or brown sugar, 30 g (1 oz) butter, and 1 teaspoon aniseed, adding some salt and pepper. Put the lid on and simmer gently for 10 to 15 minutes, when they will be cooked yet crisp and slightly candied.

Caraway Seed

(Carum carvi) Umbelliferae

Caraway is a biennial plant, native to the Mediterranean shores and now indigenous all over Europe. It is grown largely for the aromatic seeds, but the roots are also edible, being boiled and eaten like carrots. The German name for caraway is *Kümmel*, the well-known liqueur of this name having oil of caraway in its composition.

Caraway seed is very good for the digestion, and is the reason why it is traditionally included in, or eaten with, certain food. Florence White explains this very clearly in *Good English Food:*

"Roasted apples eaten with caraway comfits are a homely early eighteenth century preventative of many of the ills that flesh is heir to.

"An old gentleman of over eighty wrote in 1714 that he had eaten a roasted apple with caraway comfits every night for fifty years, and had never suffered from constipation, gout, or stone or any other distemper incident to old age.

"The custom is a much older one, dating back to the time of ancient Greece and Rome, and is probably the origin of the old saying: 'An apple a day keeps the doctor away.'

"Apples are apt to cause flatulence, for which caraway seeds and comfits give relief, and it was the custom of our ancestors to serve a dish of baked apples and caraway comfits after a meal."

There are many other virtues atttributed to caraway: it was put into love potions; and Dioscorides, the great Greek physician who lived in the first century AD, prescribed it for "girls of pale face".

Caraway seed is used in breads, particularly rye. Certain cheeses are flavoured with caraway, and it is the ingredient which gives seed cake its name. Caraway seed also flavours pickles, soups, vegetables, and meat and fish dishes.

Caraway · Rice · Ring · and · Tuna

A tasty meal for meatless days. The moulded rice looks colourful and attractive.

One 500 g tin tuna	600 ml (1 pint) milk
60 g (2 oz) butter or	2 cups rice
margarine, and 2 extra	1 dessertspoon caraway seed
tablespoons	60 g (2 oz) red caviar
1 heaped tablespoon plain flour	1 1/2 tablespoons dried parsley
1 dessertspoon paprika	Salt and pepper

Melt 60 g (2 oz) butter in a saucepan, blend in the flour and paprika, and mix to a paste. Gradually add the milk, season with salt and pepper, and add the tuna. Keep hot.

Put the rice into a quantity of boiling salted water, and when cooked drain it in a colander, running some hot water over it to separate the grains. Shake well, turn into a bowl, fold in extra butter (melted), also caraway seeds, caviar, and parsley. Turn into a ring mould, press the rice in firmly, then unmould immediately onto a large platter. Pour some of the hot tuna into the centre of the ring, and the rest around it. Serve at once.

Seed · Sponge · Cake

Seed cakes were made in some parts of England at least four hundred years ago, at the end of the wheat-sowing season.

3 eggs, separated	1 tablespoon orange-flower
140 g (5 oz) castor sugar	water (from the Continental
1 cup self-raising flour	delicatessen)
1 1/2 tablespoons cornflour	2 tablespoons water
1 dessertspoon butter	1 tablespoon caraway seed
	A pinch of salt

Beat the egg whites until stiff and dry, and make a stiff meringue by gradually adding the sugar and beating until the grains are dissolved. Gently mix in the egg yolks. Sift the flour, salt, and cornflour together three times and fold this lightly into the egg and sugar mixture. Heat together the butter, orange-flower water, and water, and fold it into the flour mixture at once together with the caraway seed. Pour into a well-greased and floured tin, sprinkle the top with castor sugar, and bake in a moderately hot oven (200°C or 400°F) for 20 minutes.

Pineapple · and · Cheese · in · the Shell

Cut a large ripe pineapple cleanly in half lengthwise through the green top, and scoop out the flesh, discarding the core. Chop the flesh into cubes, put into a bowl, and add 1 cup sugar and 1 tablespoon of sherry. Cover and leave for an hour or so. Chop 250 g (½ lb) mild Cheddar cheese into cubes and add to the pineapple, then stir in 1 tablespoon of caraway seed. Spoon into the pineapple shells, and chill.

Cardamom Seed

(Amomum cardamomum) Zingiberaceae

Cardamom is a perennial plant originating from India. It is valued for the small irregularly shaped seeds which have a strong, cool, eucalyptus-scented flavour. Cardamom is an ingredient in Indian curry powder blends, and in other forms of Indian cooking. It is also popular in Scandinavian cookery.

A delicious Indian pudding was prepared for us one day from some quite ordinary ingredients combined with exotic ones to give an exquisite appearance and distinctive flavour. It was simply a rice pudding called *Kheer*; the

milk, rice, and sugar were soaked together, then cooked in a double saucepan with a grated carrot. When the rice was cooked, cracked cardamom seed was added, the rice mixture was put into a glass dish and covered with gossamer-thin sheets of pure silver, then finished with a pattern of shelled almonds shaved thinly. It was eaten cold, and the taste was cool and aromatic: a sensible dessert to eat in a hot country and probably following a spicy curry dish. The silver seemed to melt in the mouth, and in fact when a tissue-wrapped bundle of silver sheets was produced to demonstrate the fine texture, on handling, it was so ephemeral that it appeared to float away. Only gentle and practised fingers could succeed in creating the finished effect we saw. In India, gold leaf is used as well for puddings on special occasions.

Cardamom seed is very hard and needs to be cracked by pressing the required amount with a rolling pin before using it. Blend it into the curry powder, or put a teaspoon into a pastry mixture before adding the liquid; use it in gingerbread, in coffee cake, in fruit dishes, and in rice pudding. Crush a few seeds and put them in a small bowl to be handed with coffee crystals for black coffee.

Baked · Pears · and · Cardamom

When fruit is baked in the oven, especially in wine or in a liqueur, it has a better flavour than when cooked on top of the stove.

Peel, slice, and core pears, lay them in a shallow ovenproof dish, sprinkle with sugar, and add 2 tablespoons wine or liqueur. (A Tia Maria which has a chocolate flavour was used successfully on one occasion.) Sprinkle with 2 teaspoons of cracked cardamom seed. Bake in a moderate oven (175°C or 350°F) until the pears are soft. Allow to cool. Serve with a little thick cream: the flavour of this dish must not be lost by drowning it with too much cream or custard.

Cardamom · Honey · Dressing

A delicious and nourishing dressing for fruit salad, melons, waffles, or corn cakes.

Beat 600 ml (½ pint) clear honey in an electric mixer until it is light in colour. Gradually add 2 tablespoons lemon juice and a few drops of orange-flower water. Stir in ½ teaspoon cracked cardamom seed. Keep in a screw-top glass jar.

Iced · Beetroot · and · Cardamom Salad

This method of cooking beetroots seems to preserve the goodness and flavour, and as Mrs Beeton observes, without "loss of their beautiful colour".

Place 4 large beets in a dish and bake in a slow oven for about 3 hours. Cool slightly, peel and slice thinly. Sprinkle with sugar, a little salt, and 2 teaspoons cracked cardamom seed. Pour French dressing (page 76) over, and chill thoroughly.

Celery Seed

(Apium graveolens) Umbelliferae

Celery seed is the dried fruit of the celery plant, thought to be native to Europe. However, it is said that originally it was the pot-herb known as smallage, which is wild celery: indeed, many of today's cultivated vegetables were once the simple pot-herbs of our forebears. Culpeper describes smallage in his *Complete Herbal* thus: "The roots are about a finger thick, wrinkled, and sinking deep in the earth, of a white colour, from which spring many winged leaves of a yellow colour...the roots, leaves, and seed are used."

Mrs C. F. Leyel says that celery juice "is an anti-acid tonic and stimulant rich in volatile oils and fruit sugar. It is a simple and effective remedy for some rheumatic complaints." It is interesting to read from quite another source that celery has the property to help rheumatism. Here is a recipe from *Lotions and Potions*: "Boil 1 oz [30 g] of celery seed in 1 pint [600 ml] of water until reduced to half. Strain, bottle and cork carefully. Take 1 teaspoonful twice a day in a little water for a fortnight. Repeat again if required."

Celery seed is small and brownish, and has a potent taste. It is probably one of the most popular flavourings on the spice shelf. It goes into tomato juice and seafood cocktails; in pickles and chutney; on top of breads and rolls; in soups, stews, fish dishes, and nearly all vegetable dishes; in white sauces and mayonnaise; and in cheese and herb-butter mixtures. Commercial celery salt is flavoured with ground celery seed, or with ground dried celery stems.

Cabbage · Aspic

4 cups finely shredded cabbage
2 cups chopped celery
1 red capsicum, thinly sliced
1 tablespoon celery seed
4 tablespoons gelatine

1 cup sugar
4 cups cold water
2 cups very hot water
1 cup cider vinegar
Salt
Freshly ground pepper

Green and glistening, this salad is a crisp and delicious accompaniment to a main meat course.

Pour the 2 cups of very hot water (just off the boil) onto the gelatine and sugar, and stir until both are dissolved. Add the 4 cups of cold water and the vinegar, and leave until cool, but not set. Stir in the rest of the ingredients, and pour into a rinsed-out mould. When set, unmould onto a bed of fresh herbs or lettuce leaves.

Sharp · Mayonnaise

To be eaten with cold meat.

Mix together 1 cup mayonnaise, ¼ cup prepared horseradish, and 2 teaspoons of celery seed.

Aromatic · Sweet · Potatoes

Peel and slice 500 g (1 lb) sweet potatoes and arrange in a buttered ovenproof dish. Top with slices of rindless bacon and halved pineapple rings, and sprinkle with brown sugar, freshly ground pepper, and 2 teaspoons celery seed. Bake in a moderate oven (175°C or 350°F) for 40 or 45 minutes. Serve with meat casserole, grills, or baked veal.

Coriander Seed

(Coriandrum sativum) Umbelliferae

Coriander is an annual with pink-tinged, delicately lacy flowers. It is native to southern Europe and the Near East and grows to sixty centimetres (two feet) in height. It is one of the oldest herbs known to man. In the Bible the seed is likened to manna, tasting ". . . like wafers made with honey". Today it is grown in many parts of the world.

Coriander was said by many of the early herbalists to associate well with chervil and dill, which blossom at the same time; this suggestion is also probably intended to carry out the interesting theory that certain plants are sympathetic to each other, one strengthening the other with special properties, perhaps by giving off an odour unpleasant to insects which would otherwise attack the vulnerable plant growing next to it; in return, this plant would contain qualities lacking in the other.

Coriander seeds are small, slightly oval, and bleached-looking, with an agreeable spicy flavour. Unfortunately the seed is susceptible to weevils and is therefore not easy to obtain; perhaps the best way of having it is to grow it oneself. As the seeds have the power of remaining fertile for up to five years, there is no need to worry over fresh supplies for planting. When the flowers have fallen, collect the ripe seed and store in an airtight jar: the fragrance improves with keeping.

Coriander seed is an ingredient in curry blends; it is popular in some Spanish food and in many Eastern dishes; it flavours cheese, breads, rolls, cakes, and pastries and is frequently used in sausages, preserves, and confections.

Arabian · Stuffed · Capsicums

12 medium-sized green capsicums
2 cups stock (may be made with 2 soup cubes)
2 cups cooked, chopped lamb, or 500 g (1 lb) minced steak
2 cups cooked rice
2 tablespoons skinned, slivered almonds

2 onions, chopped
2 teaspoons crushed coriander seed
½ teaspoon ground cinnamon
2 tomatoes, peeled and diced
1 tablespoon chopped olives
Salt and pepper

Prepare the capsicums for stuffing by removing a piece from the top of each and scooping out the seeds. Mix together the lamb, rice, onion, almonds, coriander seed, cinnamon, tomato, and olives, seasoning with a little salt and pepper. Stuff the capsicums, place in a baking dish, replace capsicum tops, cover with the stock, and bake in a moderate oven (175°C or 350°F) for 1 hour, basting frequently. If any meat mixture is left over, form it into balls and put them in the dish too.

Coriander · Apple · Crumble

Cover the bottom of a buttered shallow ovenproof dish with peeled, sliced cooking apples, sprinkle with 1 tablespoon raw sugar and 1 teaspoon ground cinnamon. In a bowl rub together until crumbly 1 cup plain flour, ½ cup raw sugar, and 125 g (¼ lb) butter. Press and smooth this on top of the apples, then sprinkle with crushed coriander seed (try 1 teaspoon to begin with, and increase the amount next time you make this dessert, if you wish). Bake in a moderate oven (175°C or 350°F) for about 30 minutes. Serve hot or cold with cream.

Coriander · Honey · Cakes

500 g (1 lb) honey
125 g (¼ lb) butter
500 g (1 lb) plain flour
4 tablespoons milk

1 teaspoon carbonate of soda
2 teaspoons crushed coriander
  seed

Put the honey and butter together in a saucepan and heat till bubbling. Cool a little, and pour into a bowl. Sift the flour and soda into the honey mixture, add the milk, then the crushed coriander seed. Chill, then turn onto a floured surface, form into cakes, and bake on greased and floured trays in a moderately hot oven (200°C or 400°F) for 15 minutes. Allow to cool on trays. Store in containers.

Cumin Seed

(Cuminum cyminum) Umbelliferae

Cumin is a small annual sun-loving herb, native to Egypt. The pale-pink flowers are followed by parchment-coloured seeds, the flavour of which almost holds the key to the pungent taste of curry powder. Some say that this seed resembles caraway in flavour; the seeds of both are very aromatic, but to my mind so essentially different that one could not easily replace the other. Cumin is mentioned in the Bible, the seed having been valued for the digestion, as well as for culinary purposes, for many centuries.

Cumin seed is used mainly in the blending of curry powder, chili powder, and in flavouring dishes from the Near and Middle East. A teaspoon or two of the mildly hot seed gives an Eastern flavour to food: it is often used in rye bread; in pickles and chutney; in rice, cabbage, and bean dishes; in meat dishes; and to mash into cottage cheese with a little lemon juice for a spread or dip.

Turkish · Cucumbers

4 cucumbers
1 carton yoghurt
1 clove of garlic, finely chopped

1 teaspoon salt
1 tablespoon white vinegar
1 teaspoon cumin seed
1 teaspoon chopped mint

Soak the garlic, salt, and vinegar together. Strain. Peel the cucumbers and slice them thinly lengthwise. Put the yoghurt in a bowl and stir in gradually the strained vinegar. Add the cumin seed. Pour the dressing over the cucumbers, sprinkle with mint, and serve slightly chilled.

Lamb · Shanks · Armenian

6 lamb shanks
2 tablespoons plain flour
2 cloves of garlic, finely chopped
1 onion, chopped
1 capsicum, chopped
2 teaspoons cumin seed

1 teaspoon black peppercorns
1 tablespoon lemon juice
1 dill cucumber, sliced
3 cups tomato juice
Salt

Roll the shanks in the flour and place in a large casserole with the other ingredients. Put the lid on, and bake in a slow oven (135° to 150°C or 275° to 300°F) for 2½ hours. Serve hot with brown rice and plenty of the savoury liquid.

Cumin · and · Rose · Geranium · Drops

170 g (6 oz) butter
1 cup sugar
2 eggs
3 cups self-raising flour

2 teaspoons cumin seed
Rose geranium jelly (page 43)
or other preserve
A pinch of salt

To make these fragrant confections, cream the butter and sugar, beat in the eggs one at a time, fold in the sifted flour and salt, and add the cumin seed. Form into small balls with the hands, roll in sugar, make a depression in the centre of each, and fill with rose geranium jelly. Bake in a moderate oven (190°C or 375°F). Cool on a tray and store in an airtight container.

Dill Seed

(*Anethum graveolens*) *Umbelliferae*

Dill is an annual plant, a native of southern Europe. Many centuries ago it found its way, like numerous other herbs, to the colder parts of Europe, where it became an attractive and useful wayside "weed". Today it grows in countries all over the world. The name stems from the Norse word *dilla*, meaning to lull: dill water, a decoction made from the seeds, was given to babies to soothe them in those far-off days, just as it is today. Yellow-flowering dill, very like fennel in appearance, is grown for its fresh, fern-like leaves and for the aromatic buff-coloured seeds which give food added flavour and make it more easily assimilated. It is more than coincidence that dill is put with cucumbers in the making of dill pickles, for this vegetable has the reputation of being rather indigestible. It is also one of the most appropriate herbs to use in coleslaw and in steamed cabbage. If caraway seed is not popular with some people, dill seed may be substituted, for the flavour though similar is not as strong as that of caraway.

According to a charming American leaflet about herbs, dill and fennel seed were known as "meetin' seed", having been given to children to eat during long Sunday sermons.

Dill seed is sprinkled on breads, rolls, and apple pie; it is used in sauces for vegetables and fish; it goes into stews and soups; in the pot with vegetables which need the minimum of water during cooking, such as shredded cabbage and finely sliced chokoes; it flavours pickles, chutney, potato salad, and sauerkraut; and is often cooked with veal, pork, and kidneys.

Dill · Sauce

1 1/2 cups white sauce
1 tablespoon sherry

1 medium-sized dill cucumber, diced
2 teaspoons dill seed

To be eaten with any fried fish.

Mix the sherry into the hot white sauce, blend well, and add the cucumber and dill seed. Serve hot.

Dill · Cheese · Dip · or · Spread

One small packet of cream cheese
2 tablespoons thin cream
2 teaspoons dill seed

2 teaspoons lemon juice
1 tablespoon grated onion
Salt and pepper

Blend the cheese and cream together, then add the rest of the ingredients, and mix well.

Hot · Slaw

4 cups finely shredded cabbage
2 eggs
1/4 cup water
2 tablespoons lemon juice

1 tablespoon sugar
2 teaspoons dill seed
1 tablespoon butter or margarine
Salt and pepper

Break the eggs into a saucepan and whisk with a wire whisk. Add the water, lemon juice, sugar, and dill seed, season with a little salt and pepper, and whisk well again. Place on a low flame, add the butter, and stir with a wooden spoon until the mixture thickens. Stir in the cabbage, coating thoroughly. Serve hot.

Fennel Seed

(Foeniculum vulgare dulce) Umbelliferae

Fennel is another native from Mediterranean countries. Long ago it was taken to other lands by the Romans, and today it is widely grown in most parts of the world. The two best-known varieties are perennial fennel and the annual Florence fennel. The former kind grows tall and feathery, and in early autumn its massed golden flowers foam along country roadsides; the leaves are not as tender and delicately flavoured as those of the annual fennel, which is a lower-growing type with bulbous, edible stems, a little like a squat celery in appearance. Fennel seed comes from both of these kinds, but if you are growing your own, it is suggested that Florence fennel is the wiser choice, since all parts of the plant may be used. The broad white stems should be sliced thinly and added to green salads; they are crisp and nutty, and the flavour bears a strong resemblance to that of aniseed, as in fact do all parts of this herb. The leaves are traditionally an accompaniment to fish, either in a sauce, or to be cooked with it. When the plant has finished flowering, and the heads are heavy with seed, collect and store the seeds.

Fennel is mentioned in the early Anglo-Saxon herbals; it was regarded as one of nine sacred herbs, and its properties were said to have great physical benefits and to guard against unseen evil. One of its ancient uses was for the restoration of eyesight; another use was as a decoction "to make those more lean that are too fat".

Chaucer mentions fennel:

> *Downe by a little path I fond*
> *Of mintes full and fennell greene.*

Shakespeare too knew fennel well:

> OPHELIA: There's fennel for you, and columbines; there's rue for
> you; and here's some for me; we may call it herb of grace o' Sundays.

Fennel is represented in Shakespeare's birthplace garden; the plant list is long and reads like poetry; amongst the medlars and mints grow bay trees, box, and briar; columbine, cuckoo-buds, elder, and fennel; savory, sedge, thyme, and many more.

Longfellow describes tall, perennial fennel in "The Goblet of Life":

Above the lowly plants it towers,
The fennel, with its yellow flowers,
And in an earlier age than ours
Was gifted with the wondrous powers,
Lost vision to restore.

Today fennel is considered as a useful flavouring for food, and the seed goes into breads and cakes, on top of rolls and fruit tarts, and in cheese mixtures and spreads. It gives an aromatic taste to fish dishes, and also to meat dishes, especially pork, liver, and kidneys; it goes into pickles and sauces, and is an ingredient in some curry blends.

Fennel · Tea

Boil 600 ml (½ pint) water with 1 teaspoon fennel seeds for 5 minutes. Strain.

Kidneys · and · Mushrooms

6 sheep's kidneys	*1 teaspoon paprika*
60 g (2 oz) butter	*300 ml (½ pint) stock (may be*
1 clove of garlic, chopped	*made with a soup cube)*
1 onion, chopped	*One 250 g tin mushrooms*
1 rounded tablespoon plain	*1 scant dessertspoon fennel seed*
flour	*Salt and pepper*

Melt the butter in a heavy frying pan, and soften the garlic and onion in it. Skin the kidneys, slice them, and put them into the pan. Cook gently, turning them. Stir in the flour, allowing it to brown slightly, then add the paprika, stock, mushrooms, and fennel seed. Stir until the sauce has thickened, adding salt and pepper to taste. Serve hot with buttered toast.

Fennel · Seed · Potato · Cake

A new and tasty way with potatoes is always welcome. This dish is very little trouble to prepare. Peel and slice 500 g (1 lb) potatoes thinly, butter a baking dish and put in a layer of potatoes, 1 teaspoon fennel seed, and some salt and freshly ground pepper. Dot with butter. Repeat. Finish by pouring 150 ml (¼ pint) thin cream over the top. Bake in a moderate oven (175°C or 350°F) for about 1 hour. If becoming too crisp around the edges, cover with a piece of brown paper. Test with a fork: when soft in the centre, the potato cake is cooked. Serve hot.

Juniper Berries

(Juniperus communus) Coniferae

These are the fruit of a small, evergreen tree, native to Europe, northern parts of Africa, and Arctic regions. After the berries ripen they are picked and dried. While the berries are ripening from green to silvery purple, new small cones are forming on the tree at the same time.

The resinous, sweetly sharp flavour of juniper berries not only gives a delightful smell and taste to food, but an oil from the berries is used medicinally for the treatment of kidney and digestive complaints; the aromatic globes also provide the flavouring in the manufacture of gin.

In France, juniper berries are included in many stews, while in Germany they are considered an excellent addition to sauerkraut and coleslaw. These berries are almost essential with game dishes, such as duck, grouse, quail, hare, rabbit, and venison; they are equally delicious in a stuffing for the domestic fowl, duck, goose, or turkey. Six to nine berries are usually sufficient to give the desired flavour, and they should be crushed first with the back of a wooden spoon: this is easy to do because they are soft.

Chicken · Juniper

This recipe allows 4 or 5 good servings. If you want enough for 6 to 8 people, cook two chickens and double the quantity of the ingredients.

Duck may be cooked in the same way, substituting the mixed herbs for sage in the stuffing.

One 1500 g (3 lb) chicken,	*A little grated lemon rind*
cleaned and ready to cook	*300 ml (½ pint) white wine*
¾ cup soft breadcrumbs	*2 carrots, thinly sliced*
2 teaspoons mixed herbs	*2 shallots, thinly sliced*
9 to 12 juniper berries	*1 tablespoon butter*
Salt and pepper	

Combine the breadcrumbs, mixed herbs, slightly crushed juniper berries, salt, pepper, and lemon rind, and stuff the chicken. Spread the butter over the chicken and place it in a baking dish. Pour in the white wine and add the carrot and shallot. Cover the chicken with foil and bake in a moderate oven (190°C or 375°F) for about 1½ hours (lower the heat while cooking, if necessary). To serve, lift the chicken onto a hot plate and pour the juices and vegetables over it. Buttery jacket-potatoes make a good accompaniment—they may be baked on a separate shelf in the oven at the same time. Pass round a green salad.

Juniper · Sauerkraut

One 440 g tin or fresh
  sauerkraut
300 ml (½ pint) stock
1 onion, chopped
1 clove of garlic, chopped
1 apple, chopped

60 g (2 oz) butter or
  margarine
1 cup yoghurt, sour cream, or
  thick cream
5 to 8 juniper berries, crushed
1 teaspoon celery seed

Soften the onion, garlic, and apple in the butter over a low heat, add the crushed juniper berries and the sauerkraut, celery seed, and stock. Simmer for a few minutes. Cover and put in a slow oven (150°C or 300°F) for 45 to 60 minutes. At the last stir in the yoghurt or cream. Serve hot with grilled pork, veal, or sausages.

Veal · Gruyère

1 kg (2 lb) veal fillets
2 large onions, chopped
2 cloves of garlic, chopped
125 g (4 oz) butter
12 juniper berries, crushed

One 250 g packet of sliced
  Gruyère cheese
Soft breadcrumbs
Salt and pepper

Gently fry the onion and garlic in the butter until soft. Add the crushed juniper berries and a little salt and pepper. Transfer to a baking dish, lay the veal fillets on top of the onion, then add the slices of Gruyère cheese. Sprinkle thickly with breadcrumbs and bake in a moderate oven (175°C or 350°F) for 45 minutes.

Mustard Seed

(Brassica alba) Cruciferae

Mustard is an annual herb, native to Europe, Asia, and North Africa. It is interesting to note that there are no poisonous plants in the order Cruciferae (so called because the flower petals resemble a Greek cross). Mustard is only one of many well-known plants belonging to this family: among them are such familiar flowers, herbs, and vegetables as sweet alyssum, candytuft, wallflowers, woad, cress, horseradish, and cauliflower.

Tender young leaves of mustard and cress are old favourites together as salad and garnishing herbs. Mustard greens make an excellent salad on their own: as the larger leaves are quite hot they make an interesting contrast to certain foods. The leaves are an aid to health as well, and are still thought by many people to be a help in clearing the blood.

Mustard poultices and foot-baths, also still highly thought of, are ancient remedies for colds, fevers, and sciatica.

The mustard plant reaches over a metre (3 feet) in height and produces bright yellow flowers, followed by seed which may be dark red or, in the species *alba*, light yellow. In commerce both are blended together, sometimes with turmeric, to make powdered mustard. Another commercial form is a paste consisting of mustard powder, vinegar, sugar, and herbs; the ingredients added to the powder vary with each manufacturer. Whole mustard seed is extremely palatable, and may be used when the powder or paste will not do. One expects the seeds to be too hot to eat, but they are pleasantly nutty to bite on, the released flavour having only a mild tang of mustard.

Use mustard seed with discretion to begin with, increasing the amount
as you become used to it. It goes into white sauce, mayonnaise, potato salad,
coleslaw, steamed cabbage, herb butter (page 24), cheese dishes, and
savoury spreads; it is used in fish, chicken, pork, and veal dishes, and is
recommended for sprinkling over any salted meat while boiling; it is also a
valuable addition to pickles and chutney. Lemon and Mustard Seed Chutney,
the first recipe given below, is one of the most refreshing of preserves to eat
with cold meat and curries, and to pass round at barbecues, the only
drawback being that because of its popularity the whole batch disappears too
quickly!

Lemon · and · Mustard Seed Chutney

4 medium-sized onions	*1 teaspoon ground allspice*
5 big lemons	*30 g (1 oz) mustard seed*
30 g (1 oz) common salt	*500 g (1 lb) sugar*
600 ml (1 pint) cider vinegar	*125 g (¼ lb) seedless raisins*

Peel and slice the onions, cut up the lemons (discard pips), sprinkle with the
salt, and leave for 12 hours. Add the remaining ingredients, bring to the boil, and
simmer until tender (about 45 minutes). Spoon into jars and seal when cool.

Fillets · of · Fish · Meunière

Place 125 g (¼ lb) butter in the oven in a baking dish, and when it is melted
and sizzling, put in the fillets (dipped in milk and coated with fine breadcrumbs),
and sprinkle them with salt, pepper, and 2 teaspoons mustard seed. Bake for 40 to
60 minutes in a moderate oven (175°C or 350°F), basting occasionally. If becoming
dry, add more butter. Serve hot, pouring any excess butter over the fish. A large
translucent grape, peeled, pipped, and resting on each fish, is an attractive garnish.

Ham · and · Sweet · Potato · Pie

750 g (1½ lb) ham	*2 teaspoons mustard seed*
500 g (1 lb) sweet potatoes	*2 tablespoons raw or brown*
1 large onion	*sugar*
300 ml (½ pint) or 1 tin	*A little butter*
onion soup	*Salt and pepper*

Slice the ham, cut it into pieces, and put it into an ovenproof dish. Peel the sweet potatoes and the onion, slice thinly, and put in layers over the ham, sprinkling each layer with mustard seed, salt, and pepper. Pour in the onion soup. Sprinkle the top with brown sugar, dot with butter, cover and bake in a moderate oven (175°C or 350°F) for about 1 hour.

The ham may be replaced with cold corned beef, or with cold cooked salted mutton.

Poppy Seed
(Papaver rhoeas) Papaveraceae

The slate-blue poppy seed used for cooking is produced from an annual poppy that is native to Asia and came centuries ago to Europe, where it grows wild in great abundance. These attractive plants are often seen in herbaceous borders with other old-fashioned herbs and flowers, and most of us are familiar with the many colourful varieties, both annual and perennial, which have been evolved for decorative garden displays.

Poppy seed is free of narcotic content, and so is the valuable oil extracted from the seed: opium is obtained from the unripe heads of the poppy, *Papaver somniferum*. Morphine is a valuable product of opium. Of poppy's other medicinal virtues, Florence Ranson in *British Herbs* says: "Poppy-heads have long been a rural remedy for toothache, neuralgia and other nervous pains, and once it was common to see bunches of the dried heads hanging in chemists' shops." An infusion known as "the soporific sponge", made from poppy, mandrake, hemlock, and ivy, and poured over a sponge to be held under the nostrils, was highly regarded in the Middle Ages as an anaesthetic.

Poppy seed is used extensively in European and in Eastern cooking. The tiny grains are a natural source of minerals, and are so pleasant to use in food that a jarful in the kitchen is almost indispensable. The seed may be used whole or ground. When ground it is combined with eggs, mixed candied fruit, sugar, and spice to make a nourishing fat-free and flour-free cake; a rich filling of ground poppy seed and other ingredients is made for strudels and ring cakes.

Whole poppy seed has a vast number of uses; it is sprinkled on breads, rolls, cakes, pies, mashed potato, and whipped cream; it is excellent in white sauce for vegetables, and in honey dressing for fruit; it is mixed with cooked noodles and butter, or with macaroni.

Continental · Poppy · Seed · Cake

1 1/2 cups poppy seed
6 eggs, separated
1 cup sugar

1/2 cup mixed candied fruit-peel
1 teaspoon allspice

Grind the poppy seed in a grinder or electric blender, or have it ground at a Continental delicatessen. The seeds may sometimes be bought already ground. Beat the egg yolks until thick, and while still beating gradually add the sugar. Stir in the mixed peel, allspice, and ground poppy seed. Beat the egg whites until stiff but not dry, and fold carefully and thoroughly into the poppy seed mixture. Have ready a buttered and lightly floured spring-form cake tin, and pour in the cake mixture. Put it into a preheated slow to moderate oven (160°C or 325°F) and bake for about 50 minutes. Allow the cake to cool in the tin, then carefully remove the spring-form. Spread the top of the cake with whipped cream before serving.

Alexandra's · Fruit · and · Poppy · Seed Pudding — Country · Style

1 1/2 cups self-raising flour
1/2 cup sugar
A lump of butter

Milk
1 tablespoon poppy seed
1 cup mixed candied fruit-peel

A good neighbour, Alexandra, once baked and gave me this pudding when we were very busy. It was popular with every member of the family.

Rub the butter into the flour and sugar, and add enough milk to allow the mixture to be spread into a buttered ovenproof dish. Cover with the fruit peel and poppy seed, pressing well down, then sprinkle with a little sugar. Bake in a moderate oven (190°C or 375°F). Eat hot or cold with cream.

Poppy · Seed · Noodles

To accompany grills, casseroles, rissoles, sauerbraten, goulash, stews, or meat loaf.

Put a quantity of water into a large saucepan with a pinch of salt and bring to the boil. Empty a packet of noodles into the saucepan. Continue boiling for about 15 minutes, or until the noodles are soft, stirring occasionally to prevent them sticking together. Drain in a colander, running hot water over them. Shake the noodles well and stand them on one side. Rinse and dry the saucepan, put 1 dessertspoon butter in and return it to the stove. Add the well-drained noodles and 1 tablespoon poppy seed. Reheat, mixing well together. Serve immediately.

Sesame Seed

(Sesamum indicum) Pedaliaceae

Sesame is an annual herb that is grown as an important food crop in many parts of the world today. It grows a metre (three to four feet) high and bears white flowers that are followed by oil-bearing seeds high in protein and mineral content. The mature pods pop at the merest touch, scattering the small white seeds, and this makes harvesting with machinery difficult, though strains are now being grown that do not have this tendency.

Sesame is one of the earliest and most valuable herbs known to man. The name itself is associated with well-known fables, bringing to mind Ali Baba's magic words "Open, Sesame!" and the revealing of that glowing, jewel-filled cave.

Dorothy Bovée Jones says in *The Herbarist*: "There is some disagreement among authorities as to the exact center of origin for this ancient herb. It may have been Afghanistan, or Africa, or the Sunday Islands in the East Indies. It does not exist in a wild state today. It is mentioned in Sanskrit literature and in Egyptian scripts as well as in old Hebrew writings. Marco Polo wrote that he had had sesame oil in travelling through Persia, and thought it had a better flavour than any oil he had ever tasted." Cleopatra, wise in the art of cosmetics, supposedly used sesame oil as a skin beautifier.

A product of sesame seed is an edible opaque cream known as tahina, which has the consistency of honey and in taste resembles peanut butter. It is extremely popular in Arabic, Egyptian, Lebanese, and Greek food, and may be found in some Continental provision stores. Tahina mixed with cooked brown beans makes a Lebanese dish. Another favourite dish is made with cooked eggplant and tahina mashed to a paste: it is eaten cold as an hors d'œuvre with pieces of bread. Tahina is sometimes thinned with a little lemon juice to make a nutty sauce for fish and shellfish; it is also palatable and nourishing when spread straight from the container onto bread and butter.

Tahina is an ingredient in the confection named halvah, said to be Egyptian in origin and particularly popular with Greek, Syrian, and Jewish people—and with anyone else once they have tasted it. When chilled and cut into small blocks it makes an agreeable accompaniment to black coffee. Continental delicatessens keep it.

Sesame meal, which is ground sesame seed, is obtained from health-food shops; because it is so high in protein, vegetarians use quantities of it in their daily diet. The meal is used in various ways: it is sprinkled on salads and vegetables, and together with eggs and desiccated coconut it makes sustaining and pleasant-tasting little cakes.

Sesame seed and honey bars are delectable candies to be found in Continental delicatessens and cake shops. In fact, the flavour of sesame has a powerful attraction, and anything made with the seed, or any product from it, is delicious.

There are many quick and simple ways in which sesame seed may be introduced into everyday food:

Gently fry a tablespoon of sesame seed in butter until light brown, and either toss through a green salad or add to whipped potato, cream cheese, or mashed savoury avocado.

Toast the seed lightly and sprinkle it on cooked chicken and fish, cream soups, and fruit salads.

Sprinkle sesame seed on uncooked foods like scones, biscuits, cookies, rolls, or casseroles: the seed will brown during cooking.

Use sesame seed wherever you would use nuts in cooking, for a change.

Sesame · and · Oatmeal · Cookies

2 cups rolled oats	1 teaspoon salt
¼ cup sesame seed	¾ cup desiccated coconut
¾ cup raw sugar	125 g (¼ lb) butter, melted

These are popular with children. To make, mix all the dry ingredients together, add the melted butter and stir it into the mixture. Press out onto a greased and floured tray. Bake in a moderate oven (190° to 200°C or 375° to 400°F) for 30 minutes. Cut into fingers when cold.

Sesame · Seed · Salad

1 head of lettuce	2 tablespoons sesame seed
½ cup stoned black olives	Butter
2 tomatoes, quartered	French dressing (page 76)

Wash and dry the lettuce, tear the leaves and put them into a salad bowl. Add the olives and tomatoes. Gently fry the sesame seed in butter until it is golden, add to the salad, and toss well with French dressing.

Eggplant · and · Tabina · Appetizer

This is delicious when served with thin slices of rye bread. Peel and cut up an eggplant. Fry gently in butter until soft—about 10 minutes. Turn into a bowl and mash to a pulp. Add 1 teaspoon salt, 1 tablespoon lemon juice, 2 pulverized cloves of garlic, ¼ cup tahina and 1 dessertspoon chopped mint. Blend all together.

Put the mixture into a dish and chill in the refrigerator, where it will set firm.

Vanilla Bean

(*Vanilla planifolia*) Orchidaceae

The vanilla bean comes from a perennial climbing orchid, a native of Central America. The golden flowers are followed by flat pods fifteen centimetres (six inches) in length, which when dried for culinary use are black and shiny like licorice. The perfume is sweet and permeating, and no substitute is considered suitable by connoisseurs, especially in the making of such dishes as French Ice Cream.

A piece of vanilla bean about 5 centimetres (2 inches) long should be cut, slit down the centre and used in ice creams, custards, and milk puddings, and infused in the milk for cake mixtures. The piece of bean may be rinsed and used several times. A good place for storing it is in a sugar canister, where the bean scents the sugar and remains dry and clean. Some people like to keep the vanilla bean in a little cognac, but to my way of thinking the true vanilla flavour is then overpowered.

French · Ice · Cream

300 ml (½ pint) milk	*6 eggs, separated*
300 ml (½ pint) heavy cream	*½ cup sugar*
5 cm (2 inches) of vanilla bean	

This is a smooth, rich ice cream for special occasions. Split the vanilla bean, put it into a saucepan with the milk, scald on a low flame, then stand the pan on one side. Whisk the egg yolks with the sugar, add to the milk, and stir over low heat until thick. Remove from the stove while still stirring. (If it curdles, beat with a rotary beater.) Whip the cream lightly and fold it into the custard. Pour into a chilled refrigerator tray and place in the freezing compartment. Stir once or twice during freezing.

French · Ice · Cream · Aux · Abricots

Make French Ice Cream as in the preceding recipe. Have ready 60 g (2 oz) diced glacé apricots which have been soaked in ¼ cup brandy or cognac for at least 2 hours or overnight. Fold into the ice cream before freezing it. A little apricot brandy may be poured over each serving as a sauce.

Rich · Vanilla · Custard

450 ml (¾ pint) milk   *5 cm (2 inches) of vanilla bean*
Yolks of 2 eggs, and 1 whole   *2 scant tablespoons sugar*
    egg   *1 dessertspoon butter*

Split the vanilla bean and put it into a saucepan with the milk. Scald the milk, then stand the pan on one side. Beat the eggs with sugar, pour a little of the milk onto them, and return this to the saucepan. Add the butter, and stir over a low flame until thick. Take the pan off the stove and whip the contents with a rotary beater. Pour into a jug and allow to become cool.

Vanilla · Sugar

If you have an electric blender it is only a matter of seconds to make this scented sugar for sprinkling on top of custard, whipped cream, and stewed fruit, or to dust on biscuits before baking them.

Put 1 cup sugar into a blender, and break half a vanilla bean into pieces and add to the sugar. Blend on high speed until the bean is reduced to black flecks. Keep in a screw-top jar.

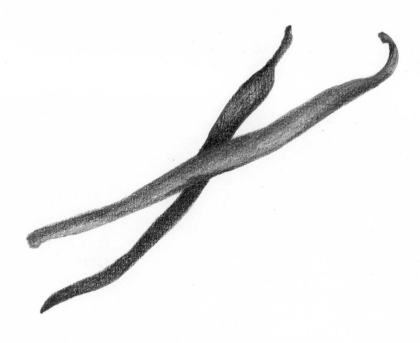

Some Books Consulted

Fragrance and Flavour Hemphill, Rosemary. Angus & Robertson, Sydney, 1959, 1961.

The Herbarist A publication of the Herb Society of America. Boston, Massachusetts, 1959.

Harmsworth's Universal Encyclopedia Educational Book Co. Ltd., London.

Island Recipe Book Compiled by M. O. Blackwell and A. M. Blandy. Vila, New Hebrides, October 1947.

The Truth About Herbs Leyel, Mrs C. F. Culpeper Press, 1954.

Lotions and Potions A little book compiled by the National Federation of Women's Institutes, England, 1956. Printed by Novello & Co. Ltd.

Mrs Beeton's Book of Household Management Ward Lock & Co. Ltd., London, 1906.

British Herbs Ranson, Florence. Penguin Books, 1941, 1954.

Herbs and Herb Gardening Rohde, Eleanour Sinclair. Medici Society, London, 1936.

A Garden of Herbs Rohde, Eleanour Sinclair. Philip Lee Warner, Publisher to the Medici Society Ltd, London. Boston, U.S.A.

Lark Rise to Candleford Thompson, Flora. Reprint Society, London, 1948.

Herbs: How to Grow Them and How to Use Them Webster, Helen Noyes. Charles T. Branford Company, Boston, revised and enlarged edition 1947.

Good English Food (Local and Regional) White, Florence. Jonathan Cape, London, 1952.

Index